The Twope

C000244391

J. Graeme B
Desmond F.

Capital Transport

First published 1996

ISBN 1 85414 186 4

Published in association with the Central Line, London Underground Ltd, by
Capital Transport Publishing, 38 Long Elmes, Harrow Weald, Middlesex

Printed by CS Graphics, Singapore

The authors and publisher would like to thank Brian Hardy, Alan A. Jackson and
Hugh Robertson for assistance with the preparation of this book.

The front cover painting is by Peter Green, GRA

The maps are by Mike Harris

CONTENTS

CENTRAL LONDON RAILWAY
As authorised in 1891
(Liverpool Street authorised 1892)

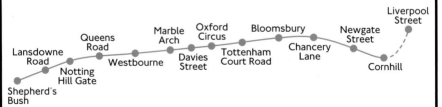

Building the Central London Railway

The great east–west traffic artery of Poultry, Cheapside, High Holborn, Oxford Street, Bayswater Road and Holland Park Avenue, served by numerous profitable horse bus routes and cutting across the middle of the Circle Line, was a natural attraction to railway promoters. Over the years from 1865 various schemes were proposed, but could hardly hope to succeed as long as they embodied the viaducts or shallow tunnels of conventional railways. In the autumn of 1889 two tube schemes were put forward. A London Central Subway would have run from Shepherd's Bush to a terminus near the present junction of New Oxford Street and Bloomsbury Street, and a Central London Railway from Queen's Road, Bayswater to a through connection with the City & South London near its terminus at King William Street. The London Central scheme fell by the wayside before reaching Parliament and the Central London was cut back to Cornhill because of CSLR opposition, and was then rejected by the House of Lords. In the following autumn the Central London promoters returned to Parliament with a proposed tube between Shepherd's Bush and Cornhill, and this time obtained sanction from both houses, with Royal Assent for the Act authorising the $5^{1}/_{2}$ mile line being granted on 5th August 1891. A further Act of Parliament, obtained in 1892, sanctioned replacement of the Cornhill terminus by one beneath the Bank intersection, and also an extension to Liverpool Street.

The Central London used an indirect method to raise capital for construction, which was copied by some later London tubes. The Exploration Co Ltd had been registered in 1889 to develop overseas mining activities and was backed by the Rothschilds. This company formed a syndicate to promote the Central London Railway, and held 21 out of the syndicate's 40 shares. The other shareholders included (Sir) Ernest Cassel (banker; friend of the financial adviser to the Prince of Wales), Henry Oppenheim (banker with overseas connections) and Darius Ogden Mills (director of numerous major New York businesses).

Cassel made repeated attempts to persuade Henry Tennant, former general manager of the North Eastern Railway, to become chairman of the Central London, and eventually succeeded on 18th June 1895, when a new board was appointed, consisting of the chairman, two members of the Prince of Wales' circle, a prominent banker and an Irish MP. The syndicate created a 'contractor', the Electric Traction Company Ltd, (formed 22nd March 1894) which agreed to build the railway for £2,544,000 plus £700,000 in 4% debentures.

Reorganisation of the board was followed, three days later, by an offer to the public of 285,000 £10 shares in the Central London Railway. The London tube railways have always had difficulty in raising capital, doubtless because of the high costs of construction and land acquisition coupled with an uncertain level of traffic receipts, and the Central London was no exception. The general public showed little interest in the offer, but Cassel and his friends took up most of the shares. Just under a quarter of them were unissued, to be taken up by the Electric Traction Company.

With finance available, the acquisition of sites began immediately, and was followed by the appointment, in spring 1896, of subcontractors to build the tunnels and the structural work – Mr J. Price for Shepherd's Bush–Marble Arch; Walter Scott & Company for Marble Arch–Post Office (now St Paul's); and Mr G. Talbot for Post Office–Bank. These worked under the technical guidance of three engineers: Sir John Fowler (1817-1898), Sir Benjamin Baker (1840-1907) and J.H. Greathead (1844-1896). Upon the death of Greathead on 21st October 1896, his duties were taken over by Basil Mott, who had been associated with him in building the City & South London. In 1898 Sir Henry Oakley resigned the general managership of the Great Northern Railway, joined the Central London board, and was appointed chairman in succession to Henry Tennant, who remained a director.

Physical construction began in April 1896 when the Chancery Lane site was cleared, to be followed by sinking a shaft there in August. By September, shafts were also being sunk at Shepherd's Bush, Lancaster Gate and British Museum, and a large space in front of the Royal Exchange had been fenced off, ready for excavation of the ticket office and sinking the lift shafts. Stations were authorised at Shepherd's Bush Green, Holland Park (shown on earlier plans as Lansdowne Road), Notting Hill Gate, Queen's Road (now Queensway), Westbourne (renamed as Lancaster Gate by the time of opening), Marble Arch, Bond Street (Davies Street), Oxford Circus, Tottenham Court Road, Bloomsbury (British Museum), Chancery Lane, Post Office (shown on earlier plans as Newgate Street and today named St Paul's) and Bank. At the last-named station, the railway company had made an agreement with the City authorities that it should build a ticket hall beneath the road intersection, surrounded by a subway forming a complete ellipse, which connected with neighbouring roads by seven subways and stairways. Upon completion, the subway system was to be opened to the public for the purpose of crossing the road as well as using the railway. After severe and expensive delays at this difficult site, which nearly bankrupted the railway, the public gained access to the majority of the subway system on 9th January 1900.

Negotiations with the Great Eastern and North London Railways for the Central London station at Liverpool Street/Broad Street were broken off at the end of 1896, but part of the authorised extension, to Old Broad Street at Throgmorton Street, was built to provide two reversing sidings.

Tunnelling followed the same general procedures that had been developed on the City & South London. Vertical shafts were sunk from station sites until they were well into the stratum of London clay. These were lined with cast iron segments and subsequently used as lift or ventilation shafts. At the foot of these shafts the tunnelling shields were assembled, and began to move horizontally to construct the running tunnels. The Greathead shields were essentially metal drums with a circular cutting edge at the front, which were propelled by a ring of hydraulic rams bearing against the last completed section of tunnel. The circular tunnels were formed of successive rings of flanged cast iron segments, each segment being bolted to its neighbour in the ring and to the next ring. The twin running tunnels were 11ft 8¼ins internal diameter, but were lined with concrete for a short distance on either side of stations, reducing the internal diameter to 11ft 6ins. A larger diameter had to be used on curves to allow for the throw-over of the bogie cars.

Station tunnels were 325ft long and 21ft 6ins internal diameter. There was a separate platform and tunnel for each direction. The standard arrangement was for the two platforms to be on the same level, connected by cross passages served by stairways. These linked with further passages from the lower landings of the lifts.

There were modified layouts at three stations, where one tunnel was above the other so that both could be under public streets and avoid paying compensation to owners of private property. At Post Office and Notting Hill Gate the westbound line was on top, but at Chancery Lane it was the eastbound. The running tunnels adjoining the stations had gradients to assist acceleration and braking. For the first 300ft leaving a station there was a down gradient of 1 in 30 (except Notting Hill Gate eastbound) and for the last 300ft approaching a station there was an uphill gradient of 1 in 60. There were larger running tunnels to house the scissors crossovers just before and just beyond each terminus of Bank and Shepherd's Bush, and there were also separate standard size reversing tunnels between the two running tunnels at Queen's Road, Marble Arch and British Museum. The Queen's Road siding was for reversing trains from the west, and the other two for trains from the east. At each site there was also a short spur for locomotives, between the connections to the two running lines.

The 1891 Act had conditionally sanctioned street improvements at Davies Street (Bond Street), but when these negotiations fell through, a Bill was deposited to acquire a new station site between the forks of Marylebone Lane at Oxford Street. However, by early 1897 negotiations were resumed, and eventually the original scheme was completed and the Bill for the alternative site withdrawn.

By the end of 1897 three quarters of the running tunnels had been completed, half the station tunnels and nearly all the lift and staircase shafts. The Shepherd's Bush depot and power station were well in hand. Twelve months later, all tunnelling had been completed except for 300ft near Bank. The 1891 Act had stipulated that the railway should be complete by 1896, so further Acts for extension of time had to be obtained, in 1894 (completion by 1899) and 1899 (completion by 1900). In 1899 most of the track was laid and a start had been made in erecting station buildings and installing lifts. In February 1899, agreement was made with the City Corporation to introduce 24-hour working on the Bank station roof and subways; the electric locomotives were delivered later that year, and the first trial run was made on 1st March 1900, between Shepherd's Bush and Queen's Road. This showed that some modifications were necessary to improve the clearances between the locomotives and the tunnels. The lower pair of cab footsteps was removed, and the bogie bolster suspension was modified.

The Prince of Wales had shown great interest in the undertaking (not surprisingly in view of the close involvement of his financial advisers) and the directors arranged for him to open the line one day before the time limit in the 1899 Act. At 3pm and 3.30pm on 27th June 1900 (nearly five weeks before public services commenced) trains loaded with special guests, viz railway representatives, financiers and Samuel Clemens (Mark Twain) left Bank for the Shepherd's Bush depot. At 3.30 His Royal Highness was received at Bank by the company chairman, Sir Henry Oakley, and at 3.36 the Prince's train began its non stop journey to Shepherd's Bush, passing the station at 3.55 and arriving at the depot at 3.58. In a marquee in the depot grounds, the Prince made a very brief speech declaring the railway open and expressing his conviction that it would be a great boon to the inhabitants of London. There was no time for further speeches, and His Highness swiftly returned eastwards, to prepare for a dinner with Mr & Mrs Bischoffsheim at their home in South Audley Street. H.Louis Bischoffsheim was a friend of Sir Ernest Cassel and had been one of the railway's main financial backers. Central London staff who had been guarding the station platforms were later allowed to go to Wood Lane to mop up the remaining refreshments, but when they arrived they found all the waiters drunk and not a drop of liquid refreshment left.

CENTRAL LONDON (TUBE) RAILWAY.

TAKING THE TICKET AT BANK STATION.

DISPOSING OF THE TICKET.

No worry about price
2ᴰ any distance

All tickets dropped into this box
No worry about losing them

SAFE & COMMODIOUS LIFTS.

TAKE **T**HE **TWO** PENNY **T**UBE

No Worry about accidents

AND **A**VOID **A**LL **A**NXIETY

SHEPHERD'S BUSH. — HOLLAND PARK. — NOTTING HILL GATE. — QUEEN'S Rᴰ. — LANCASTER GATE. — MARBLE ARCH. — BOND Sᵀ. — OXFORD CIRCUS. — TOTTENHAM COURT Rᴰ. — BRITISH MUSEUM. — CHANCERY LANE. — POST OFFICE. — THE BANK.

CENTRAL LONDON RAILWAY.

ENTERING THE TRAIN.

LEAVING THE STATION AT SHEPHERD'S BUSH.

Trains every few minutes.
No worry about catching them.

The whole distance covered so quickly
that there's nothing to worry about.

The First Modern Tube

The Central London was immediately popular with the travelling public. From opening day on 30th July 1900 until the end of that year, 14,916,922 passengers were carried. Revenue was roundly £120,000 and working expenses (at a time of high costs) £70,000. Provision for interest payments took about £10,000, leaving a surplus of nearly £40,000 for a share dividend of 2½%. A flat fare of 2d end to end applied all day but 2d workmen's returns were available in the early morning period, and the 'Twopenny Tube' soubriquet bestowed by the press soon caught on. Tickets were issued from offices outwardly resembling those of the main line railways, but were given up prior to travel.

A ride on the clean, new Central London was clearly better value for money than on the slow and expensive horse drawn buses on the streets above, and passengers flocked in. The CLR indirectly caused a decline in the umbrella trade as the city gentlemen no longer needed to protect their silk hats from rain on the open tops of buses. Tube traffic benefited from national events – the return from the Boer War of the City Imperial Volunteers in October 1900, and the Coronation of Edward VII in 1902. For the first few years the Central London was king, but on the horizon there were signs of competition from rival transport modes.

For its depot and power station the Central London was fortunate in being able to acquire a 20-acre site north of Shepherd's Bush, hitherto occupied by a fine house and garden known as Woodside Park. There was a twelve-road carriage shed 360ft long, a six-road engine shed, and locomotive and carriage repair shops. All these sheds were encircled by a loop line, at first onion shaped in plan, with the point to the north. Originally there had been proposals that some cars would be stabled overnight in selected tunnel stations, which were provided with pits between the running rails for simple inspections. This did not work well in practice, and a second twelve-road carriage shed was opened in about 1903 on the site of paved carriage-cleaning sidings. This new shed adjoined the first, on the inside of the loop. There was also a running connection from the east side of the loop to the West London Railway, which was useful for delivering new rolling stock and truckloads of coal for the power station. The loop line converged on two lines running east–west along the northern boundary – a siding forming a run-round loop, and a reception siding at the end of the connecting line from the west end of Shepherd's Bush station (westbound road).

Output from the power station, using reciprocating engines, was 5,000V three phase a.c., fed to rotary converter substations in the base of lift shafts at Notting Hill Gate, Marble Arch and Post Office. Current was transformed in two stages, to 330V a.c., then to 550V d.c. at the conductor rails. Battery stations at Queen's Road, Bond Street and Post Office provided lighting current for emergencies or after traffic hours. Surface substations to supplement the deep level installations were later added at Bond Street (replacing Marble Arch) and Post Office, and a rotary converter was installed in the power house to give a d.c. feed to Notting Hill Gate in emergency.

The General Electric Company of America (of which Darius Ogden Mills was a director) won the contract to supply the electrical equipment, i.e. the power station, distribution network and the locomotives. This was supplied through its British agency, the British Thomson Houston company, and designed by Dr Horace Field Parshall (1865-1932), electrical engineer. Greathead had intended to have a locomotive permanently coupled at each end of a train, to spread the tractive effort and to avoid locomotive shunting at termini, but the Board of Trade refused to sanction power cables running along the train because of fire risk. Therefore trains had to be hauled by a single, more powerful locomotive, and as gears and motor design had not yet developed to give the quietness and efficiency required by railway traction, these camel back locomotives had gearless motors with an armature integral with the axle. The twenty-eight locomotives were shipped to Britain in knocked down form, carried on barges from London Docks to Chelsea, and then by road to the Wood Lane sheds, where they were assembled. One locomotive was on a barge which sank after an accident, but it was successfully raised and dried out. The fleet was of Bo-Bo configuration, with two motors on each bogie and a single controller in the central cab, although with duplicate instruments for each direction of travel. They were 30ft long over buffers, and had bonnets on each side of the cabs which housed the starting resistances.

Braking was by the Westinghouse compressed air system, and there was an air compressor on each machine. Two men manned each cab, with an assistant who could take charge if the driver had a mishap, looked out for starting signals from the front guard, and dealt with the coupling and uncoupling at termini. The total weight was 44 tons, of which only about 10 tons was spring borne, since there was no axle-box suspension, only bolster springs. They were finished in crimson lake with gold lettering, lined in black edged with red (inside) and yellow (outside).

By the end of 1901 the company owned 168 trailer cars, with platforms at each end. The main car body, of teak and mahogany and strengthened with steel, was separated from the platforms by sliding doors, and the platforms had hinged gates of iron grilles on each side, under control of a gateman, to allow passengers to board and alight at stations. There was also a 3ft 4in opening at the end over the buffer beam. The clerestory roofs extended over the platforms, but weather protection was not needed at that time as the cars did not come into the open air except at the depot. Inside the saloons 48 seats were provided, with two pairs of double transverse seats on each side of the gangway in the centre (16 passengers), the other seats being longitudinal, with the individual passenger spaces being divided by heavy leather armrests. There were variations in the fittings and upholstery, partly arising from the original intention to have two classes, partly from the fact that two different bodybuilders were involved and partly because of different specifications for smoking and non-smoking cars. In smoking cars, rattan (2nd Class) or maroon haircloth (1st Class) was used for the seat coverings, while some non-smoking cars had moquette. Wooden rods, carrying straps for support of the standing load, were attached to the deck rails. Lighting was by electric incandescent lamps, and parcel racks were fitted. Car dimensions were 45ft 6ins long over platforms (39ft over bodies), 8ft 6ins wide at waist and 9ft 4^1/$_2$ins high overall. They weighed 14 tons. The Ashbury Railway Carriage and Iron Company of Manchester supplied 143 cars and the Brush Electrical Engineering Company of Loughborough 25. Externally they were finished in purple brown below the waist and white above, with 'CENTRAL LONDON' in four inch gold block letters on the waist panels, and the company's coat of arms immediately beneath.

Electric locomotives being assembled at Wood Lane sheds in 1899.
Capital Tansport collection

An original trailer car in Wood Lane sheds. The faint word 'class' on the roof may survive from the time when it was intended that the cars should have separate first and second class accommodation. Capital Transport collection

Interior of an opulently-upholstered trailer car, no doubt intended for first class and possibly part of the train used for the royal opening ceremony, as reproduced in a 1900 souvenir opening brochure.

A 'second class' version, with less elegant seating and notices asking passengers not to spit. In the event the railway opened with a single-class fare.

Left **One of the original locomotives and its train at an unidentified station.**
Commercial postcard

Below **A station stop during what may have been a trial run, judging by the absence of passengers and abundance of staff.**
Capital Transport collection

The track in the tunnel section was unusual, consisting of 100 pounds per yard bridge rail in 60ft lengths, supported by longitudinal sleepers which were embedded in concrete. Bull head rail was used at point and crossing work. The single 85lb channel section steel conductor rail was in the middle of the track, $1\frac{1}{2}$in higher than the running rails and mounted on cross timbers. Wooden extensions to the conductor rails kept the central collector shoes clear of the running rails at points and crossings. The return current flowed through the running rails, which were electrically bonded at joints.

The 325ft station tunnels had a clean but spartan appearance, with brilliant white tiling covering both sides and the ceiling vault. Station names were on large oblong enamelled iron sheets with moulded wooden frames, and lighting was by electric arc lamps. Initially the platforms were of wooden planks, having been designed before serious fires on the Liverpool Overhead Railway and the Paris Metro caused fire risks to be taken more seriously. They were replaced by stone paving slabs during the first few years of operation.

City gents waiting for lifts at Bank station in about 1900. Passengers had to drop their flat-fare tickets into a box before entering the lifts. Commercial postcard

Frank Julian Sprague, the American inventor and entrepreneur, secured the order to supply 48 electric lifts. The motors and other equipment were placed at the bottom of the lift shafts, so that the cables from the winding gear ascended to pass over pulleys at the top of the shafts, then down again to be secured to the roofs of the passenger cars. Most stations had three lifts in one shaft or four lifts in two, but Bank had five in single shafts and Post Office five in three shafts.

Above ground, all stations except Bank had surface buildings to a standard design by the architect Harry B. Measures, with external elevations of unglazed terracotta, half baked to obtain a light brown colour. These housed the ticket offices, the lift upper landings, and staff accommodation. In most cases the flat roofs eventually carried several storeys of offices or chambers, the first such extensions being designed by Delissa Joseph.

There were 17 signalboxes controlling mechanically worked semaphore starting signals and inner and outer homes with sliding spectacles, worked by wires from the boxes. Most boxes were sited on the ends of the platforms against the tunnel headwall. The three stations with platforms on two levels (Post Office, Chancery Lane and Notting Hill Gate) had one box for each direction, and there was a further one in the Wood Lane yard, near the top of the slope down to Shepherd's Bush. The main block section was from one station starting signal to an outer home about 1,800ft before the next station, and there was another block from there to the inner home. The block signals were equipped with electric lever locks. A brush on the last bogie of each train contacted an insulated copper treadle plate ahead of each home signal, releasing part of the lock and block mechanism in the signalbox.

The original provision for ventilation had been delightfully simple – it was left to the piston action of the trains in the close fitting tunnels. But this proved to be greatly over optimistic. Sir Theodore Martin, Parliamentary Agent, giving evidence to the Royal Commission on London Traffic in February 1904, said 'For myself, I could not risk my health by travelling on such a railway as the Central London, with its obnoxious vapour, which I know from meeting it at the stations . . . many individuals I know are giving it up.'

In the absence of practical experience in the ventilation of tube railways, the railway company attacked the problem by trial and error expedients, with an existing substation fan at Post Office adjusted to draw air from the platforms, and new fans at Bond Street and British Museum. A bizarre attempt to relieve the problem comprised the installation of a large fan near Wood Lane, the closure of the tunnel mouth by a hinged door, and closing the doors of all stations except Bank. The theory was that the stale air could be sucked out of the whole line, and tests showed that over one half of the air discharged at Wood Lane came in at Bank. However, the useful effect of the Bank air was exhausted before it had gone more than two miles, so the rest of the journey was needless effort. Some suggested putting pots of evergreen shrubs on the platforms, but the problem was not solved until an elaborate pressure system was installed in 1911, delivering washed and ozonised air; even this system supplied smaller amounts of air than are normal by current standards.

Almost as soon as the railway opened the occupants of nearby property complained of being disturbed by excessive vibration. In January 1901 the Board of Trade appointed a committee of experts to report and advise. Official observers were stationed in the affected premises, with seismographs, cameras and telephones to the nearest CLR signalbox. An interim report of May 1901 attributed the trouble to the large proportion of unsprung weight in the locomotives and lack of rigidity in the track. The railway promptly co-operated by converting three locomotives to geared operation with smaller, higher-speed motors in new bogies; it simultaneously converted four of the existing trailer cars to motor cars equipped for Thomson Houston multiple unit operation. These entered service in September 1901. One bogie of each car was replaced by a power bogie with two 100hp motors. The floor at one end of the car was raised to clear the motor bogie and the driver's cab was built at that end. Initially two trailers were marshalled between two experimental cars, but two further trailers were soon added to make a six-car train. The observers returned to their posts, finding that the geared locomotives caused less than one third of the vibration of the direct drive machines, but the experimental multiple unit trains produced less than a fifth. The Committee's final report of February 1902 observed that a deeper and stiffer rail would have been preferable to the bridge rails, which could not now be changed as the vertical clearances would have been too tight (for locomotives).

Three months after the report appeared, the company ordered 64 new motor cars, 24 from Brown, Marshalls & Co Ltd (which was on the point of amalgamating with four other companies to form the Metropolitan Amalgamated Railway Carriage & Wagon Co) and 40 from the Birmingham Railway Carriage & Wagon Co. These 42-seat cars had BTH manual electro-magnetic control equipment, two 125hp motors and rattan seating. They had a half-octagonal roof over the driver's cab (which could still be seen in recent years when 36 of these cars were cut up and reassembled to form 18 sleet locomotives); at the non-driving ends they had gated platforms similar to the original trailers. The complete changeover to multiple unit operation took just two months, to 8th June 1903. The company had hoped to run trains with a third motor car in the middle, but this was disallowed because of expected difficulty in detraining passengers in an emergency through the narrow equipment compartment. Heavy power cables along the train were avoided by using Frank Sprague's system of multiple unit control, whereby each motor car drew its own current from the conductor rail, and had its own set of resistances, controlled by low voltage current from a master controller manipulated by the driver.

A painting showing a scene at the Bank terminus after the replacement of the locomotives by motor cars. Commercial postcard

Six all-steel trailers were bought from the Birmingham company in 1903. The extra rolling stock required even more accommodation at the depot, and a new nine-road shed parallel to Wood Lane (and outside the loop) was built in the same year. With the introduction of multiple unit operation, there was less need for staff to walk about the depot tracks. Current rails were installed in the open section of the depot from 1903, and the overhead wires were finally eliminated in 1908.

Solving the vibration problem had left the CLR with much non-standard rolling stock. Two of the experimental motor cars were converted back to trailers, and another was used for a short time as a tunnel whitewashing car. By 1915 both of these remaining motor cars were converted to battery locomotives, for use on night-time engineers' trains, which made a start in converting the tunnel track to bull-head rail and cross sleepers. The electric locomotives were offered for sale, but little enthusiasm was shown. In 1905 the Metropolitan Railway bought two of the geared machines for regenerative control experiments, but sold them for scrap in 1915. The CLR kept one gearless and one geared loco, for yard shunting, and these were scrapped in 1928 and 1942 respectively. The other 24 locomotives were sold for scrap in about 1906, but there were reports that some found further use on industrial lines.

In order to economise in running costs, the CLR began to convert some trailer cars to 'control trailers', so that three-car trains could run in the off-peak, consisting of motor-trailer-control trailer. The conversion consisted of fitting power and brake controls on one of the platforms, and a divided end bulkhead separated by a central roller shutter (folding doors on later conversions) to provide the driver and his assistant with some rudimentary protection. It proceeded slowly, from December 1908, and ceased in December 1925 when the fleet included 72 control trailers.

The 1903 motor cars 'inherited' an unusual feature from the locomotives, in that the driving position was always on one side of the train. Cabs facing Bank had the controls on the left, and those facing Shepherd's Bush had them on the right, i.e. the driver was always on the north side of his train, corresponding to the siting of the tunnel signals.

Above
Side view of one of the 64 motor cars which entered service in 1903, in Wood Lane yard. The overhead trolley wires were used by two electric locomotives equipped with trolley poles, which shunted the trailer cars. LGRP

Left *Punch* cartoon about the twopenny flat fare.

THE TWOPENNY TUBE

"Hi, guv'nor, there ain't no station named on this ticket!"
"No; all our tickets are alike."
"Then, 'ow do I know where I'm going?"

Station building at Shepherd's Bush, with intending passengers about to strain the capacity of a London United tramcar bound for Acton. The station exterior is largely unchanged today. LT Museum

At first the trains were very labour-intensive, and eight men were carried on a seven-car train: the driver and his assistant, a front and rear guard, and four gatemen. Starting was a complicated ritual, with each gateman facing the front of the train and holding up his hand when his gates were shut. When the front guard saw the correct number of hands he showed a green light to the rear, to which the rear guard responded by showing a green light forward and blowing a whistle. On receiving these signals the front guard showed a green light forward to the driver or his assistant, and the train could start. The Central London was unique amongst London Underground railways in employing 'call boys' to call at the houses of all drivers living near Shepherd's Bush to wake them up. Conditions were harsh. Straight shifts were ten hours long, without any meal break. The cab crews brought sandwiches and left supplies of tea and sugar with the signalmen, collecting their brewed tea when next passing. Sometimes they were given a cooked bloater. At the end of the day, their faces were black from metal dust from the motors and brake blocks. In 1908 an assistant driver was paid 30 shillings (£1.50) for a 60 hour week.

Reverting briefly to the locomotive era, experience had shown that the time taken at termini to change locomotives could not be reduced below $2\frac{1}{2}$ minutes, which determined a minimum headway of $3\frac{1}{2}$ minutes (outside the peaks, the normal service interval was five minutes).

Therefore the CLR deposited a Parliamentary Bill in autumn 1900 for a loop at each end of the line. At the west end it would have been under Shepherd's Bush Green, but at the City end it could either have been entirely underneath the Great Eastern's Liverpool Street terminus, approached via Old Broad Street, or alternatively in a larger loop via Threadneedle Street, Bishopsgate and Liverpool Street, returning via Blomfield Street and Old Broad Street. Unfortunately the existence of the Central London itself helped to defeat this scheme, as its apparent financial success attracted bills for new tube railways in all parts of London. These were remitted to a parliamentary Joint Select Committee which had the duties of suggesting a new framework for London tube promotions and of selecting from the competitive bills those best suited to present and future traffic requirements. On the Central London bill, the Committee did not favour either City loop, and the bill was withdrawn, in favour of a much more ambitious scheme for the 1901-2 session. The large loop proposed in this scheme would first have extended the Central London west along Goldhawk Road, then looped round to serve Hammersmith pointing east, then continued via Kensington High Street, Hyde Park Corner, Piccadilly, Leicester Square, Strand, Fleet Street and Ludgate Circus. It then swung south to avoid St Paul's Cathedral, into New Bridge Street and left into Queen Victoria Street. On reaching Bank it would have made a large loop via Cornhill, Leadenhall Street, St Mary Axe, Liverpool Street and Old Broad Street to rejoin the existing line.

The spate of new bills was augmented even further, and they were remitted to two Select Committees. It is likely that if the Central London had been alone in seeking a Kensington–Piccadilly–Fleet Street route it would have succeeded. However, a rival scheme backed by the American financier John Pierpont Morgan would have stretched from Hammersmith to Palmers Green. This scheme was favoured because it took in suburban territory as well as inner urban, and the Central London bill was rejected. The company resubmitted its 1902 proposals in 1903 and 1905 bills, but withdrew them later. In October 1905 the CLR agreed with the Underground (Yerkes) Group that neither would submit an east–west bill in the 1906 session. By 1907 a decline in traffic and the competition from mechanical road transport caused thoughts of major extensions to be put aside. By then, the Central London had reversible multiple unit trains which, even at dead end termini, could give a 2-minute service. Trains were generally of six cars in the peak, three in the off-peak.

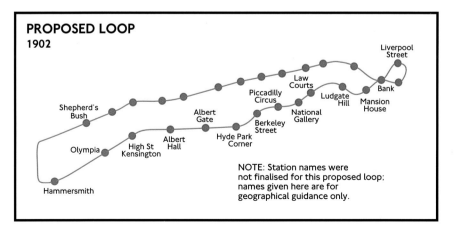

PROPOSED LOOP
1902

Liverpool Street
Law Courts
Piccadilly Circus
Bank
Shepherd's Bush
Ludgate Hill
Albert Gate
Mansion House
National Gallery
Berkeley Street
Olympia
High St Kensington
Albert Hall
Hyde Park Corner
Hammersmith

NOTE: Station names were not finalised for this proposed loop; names given here are for geographical guidance only.

First Extensions

It was fortunate for the Central London that the tides of history brought the British and French nations so closely together in the first decade of the 20th century. When, in late 1905, the French Chamber of Commerce in London suggested that the two countries collaborate in a Franco-British exhibition, the idea was eagerly taken up on both sides of the Channel. The main objective was for both countries to display and promote their industrial achievements. The task of creating such an exhibition was given to Mr Imré Kiralfy, a Hungarian immigrant who had successfully organised similar ventures at Earl's Court from 1895 to 1903, where the site was proving inadequate. Fortunately, a site of 140 acres west of Wood Lane, Shepherd's Bush was soon secured, and the first sod was cut on 3rd January 1907. The French architectural profession made a large contribution to the design of the exhibition buildings. As a kind of *hors d'oeuvre* to the main exhibition, a series of giant halls, each measuring about 400ft long and 70ft wide linked the east end of Shepherd's Bush Green to the main exhibition entrance west of Wood Lane. These were about 30ft above ground level, and dwarfed the Central London's Wood Lane depot. There was a very tall and ornate entrance to the halls in Uxbridge Road, very close to the Shepherd's Bush station of the CLR and Uxbridge Road station of the West London Railway. After walking about half a mile through these halls, visitors crossed Wood Lane by a special bridge and by-passed another entrance, in Wood Lane, lower than the other but just as elaborately finished in white plaster mouldings.

The Central London directors saw that, with relatively modest expenditure, they could extend the line to a new station opposite the second exhibition entrance, and secured authority for a second line between Shepherd's Bush and the depot by Act of 26th July 1907. The two-platform Wood Lane station was built on the site of the depot reception siding. It had a road frontage in dark reddish brown tiles, with a small shop flanked by two lattice-gated entrances. Inside there was a large ticket office in the middle of the circulating area, with lavatories and staff offices on the left.

On leaving the station, trains used a newly constructed stretch of line, parallel to the east side of Wood Lane. It entered a tunnel to pass beneath the Wood Lane sheds built in 1903 (which had a new fan of sidings added to connect the north end of the shed to the station), then passed below Bulwer Street and Aldine Street, finally crossing under the westbound running tunnel to connect into the eastbound siding and platform at Shepherd's Bush station. A revised track layout allowed trains from the depot to join the main line at the east end of Wood Lane station and leave it at the west end, but because the station tracks were lower than the original depot access road, both of the new access roads were steeply graded. The western ends of the station platforms were on a 300ft radius curve; in fact, except within the car sheds, there was scarcely a piece of straight track anywhere inside Wood Lane depot, and there was some resemblance to a model railway whose owner tries to cram tracks into every possible space.

The new loop opened on 14th May 1908, the same day as the Franco-British exhibition, which brought some welcome extra railway traffic. The exhibition buildings were of concrete on steel frames, plastered and with numerous plaster embellishments. They were painted white to protect them from the weather, and soon gained the unofficial title 'White City'. Further large and important exhibitions were held each year until 1914. The White City stadium, also opened in 1908 for the Olympic Games, had a longer-lasting effect on the Central London, as it was later used for numerous attractions, particularly greyhound racing, athletics and horse shows.

The original Wood Lane station entrance. A wide footbridge between the two gateways carried exhibition traffic. LT Museum

An enterprising exhibit by the Central London at the Imperial International Exhibition, White City, 1909, with full-sized motor car and a section of running tunnel, which contained working examples of signals and train brakes.

The loop working had the advantage that drivers did not need to change ends at this terminus. On the other hand, it turned trains round. If a train had to have a car removed and another substituted, all cars had to be the same way round, otherwise the air supply and brake pipe hoses could not be connected. To keep cars facing the right way, a turntable was installed in the yard in 1908.

At the other end of the line, it was absurd for the terminus to remain at Bank when the two main line termini of Liverpool Street and Broad Street were so close, and new Parliamentary powers were obtained on 16th August 1909 to extend the line to these stations. The Act included the curious provision that no foul air should escape from the tube into Broad Street station. The Great Eastern agreed that a tube station could be built under its property on condition that the Central London should make no further extension north or north east. Work began in July 1910 on the twin 12ft 5in tunnels under Broad Street, extending the 400ft Bank siding tunnels. Just before Liverpool Street there was a 25ft diameter tunnel for a scissors crossover. The station tunnels were 21ft 2¹/₂in diameter, and 325ft long. Beyond, there was another scissors crossover and then sidings extending to the north east corner of the main line station.

The tube platforms were connected to the Central London's subsurface ticket hall by two 'A' type (shunt type, step off sideways) escalators in single inclined shafts, the first escalators on the Central London. A third shaft, to one side, accommodated a staircase. At the southern end of the station, two further escalators in single shafts were commissioned later in the same year, running between a landing above the platforms and a ticket hall beneath Broad Street station forecourt. In 1913 Otis electric lifts linked the Central London landing and the Broad Street station concourse, but they were in passenger service for only two years. At the opening ceremony on 27th July 1912, Lord Claud Hamilton, chairman of the Great Eastern, stressed that his railway was making no charge for use of the station site as it was taking a 'broad view' that what would benefit the Central London would benefit the Great Eastern. The public opening was on the following day.

By 1907, the Central London's competitors had begun to hit back. The central London sections of the Metropolitan and District were electrified in 1905, the Piccadilly Line opened to Hammersmith in 1906, and motor buses gradually displaced the horse drawn type. Annual traffic on the CLR dropped from 43,057,997 in 1906 to 36,907,491 in 1907. To secure more revenue, the 2d flat fare was increased to 3d for longer journeys from 1st July 1907, so that the 2d fare from Shepherd's Bush now ended at Tottenham Court Road, and that from Bank at Marble Arch. However, books of twelve 3d tickets could be bought for 2s 9d. Fares for short journeys were reduced to 1d from 14th March 1909. Strips of twelve 2d tickets had been sold at no discount from opening in 1900, but in November 1908 the price was reduced to 1s 10d. In January 1910, books of fifty 3d tickets were sold for 10s 6d, and season tickets were introduced on 1st July 1911. A season ticket holder could obtain special discounts on seasons for two or more members of his family, and in January 1912 shopping season tickets were issued for ladies attending the sales.

Front and back of original style CLR flat-fare ticket, coloured lilac.

With falling receipts, economies were needed, and the assistant drivers were the first major casualties. From 1909 their services could be dispensed with as the stop signals had by then been equipped with train stops, and the driving cars with tripcocks and 'dead man's handles'. Train stops were small levers next to the track which were kept down by air pressure but automatically raised by springs when the signal was at danger, engaging with a trip arm on the car to actuate a tripcock valve which quickly released the compressed air from the braking system. This caused any train passing a signal at danger to be brought to a sudden halt. The other device included fitting springs to the handle on the master controller so that it pressed upwards. The driver had to press down continuously; if he released the handle the emergency brake would be automatically applied.

A further step in reducing the number of staff (and in increasing line capacity) was to close as many signalboxes as possible by introducing automatic electro-pneumatic signalling, whereby the trains themselves put the signals behind them to danger by means of track circuits. This was installed by McKenzie, Holland and Westinghouse, and used a.c. track circuits and two-aspect red and green colour light signals, with repeaters (with yellow for caution) where sighting was difficult. Impedance bonds were fitted at the insulated joints in the running rail at the ends of signalling block sections. These allowed the return traction current to flow across the joint but effectively stopped the a.c. signal current. Signal boxes were retained at Bank, British Museum, Marble Arch, Queen's Road and Wood Lane, but if the intermediate sidings or crossovers were not required, the signalbox there could be cut out and the main line signals worked automatically. At Shepherd's Bush, the Wood Lane extension had resulted in the simplification of the track layout to the through tracks and one trailing crossover, which was controlled by a new eleven-lever power frame. The new Liverpool Street station was equipped with an electro-pneumatic locking frame containing 12 working levers and one spare. The movable diamonds in the scissors crossovers were connected to the rods moving the point switches, and locked in position, all movements being by compressed air. In the darker parts of Wood Lane depot, colour light signals with hoods were used, but two upper quadrant stop signals were installed in the more open part. The resignalling was completed by June 1914. The opportunity was taken to site the new signals in standard positions to the left of the driver. A start was made in moving the driver's position in the cab so that it was always on the left at either end of the train, but this proceeded at a lethargic pace, and some right hand driving positions survived beyond 1928.

Some developments took place at the older stations during this period. At Bank, a low level subway to the City & South London Railway was available from opening day, but a high level subway between the ticket halls was not available until 3rd May 1911. At Tottenham Court Road, low level interchange with the Hampstead line was available from the opening of that line in June 1907, and similarly with the Bakerloo at Oxford Circus from March 1906. Passengers had to rebook at low level ticket offices until the introduction of through fares in late 1907 and early 1908 removed that need. The large store of Harry Gordon Selfridge was being built near Bond Street station in 1908, and opened on 15th March 1909. Selfridge used many innovative marketing initiatives, but his suggestion that Bond Street station be renamed Selfridge's was cold shouldered by the railway. At Shepherd's Bush the heavy passenger traffic soon outstripped the capacity of the three existing Sprague electric lifts, and two extra shafts were sunk. These were equipped with Waygood hydraulic lifts, two in December 1902 and two in February 1903.

The Central London maintained a parcels collection and delivery service from 1911 to 1917. Messenger boys on hired tricycles collected and delivered parcels, working from each station. The parcels, in wicker baskets, were taken to tube level by lift and carried in modified motor cars. LT Museum

A parcels delivery service was started in 1911, advertised as the 'Lightning Parcels Express'. Messenger boys riding hired tricycles conveyed them between nearby premises and Central London stations, and four trains were modified with special compartments in the motor cars to convey the parcels and allow them to be sorted en route. They were conveyed between surface and platform in large basketware trolleys. This service initially made a small profit, but succumbed to wartime labour shortage in 1917, never to be resumed.

Financial pressure caused the Central London directors to examine extensions into the suburbs, from where extra traffic could be drawn in to support the expensively built central section. In the autumn of 1912 they deposited a bill for an extension westwards from Shepherd's Bush station via Goldhawk Road, Stamford Brook Road, Bath Road, Chiswick Common and Chiswick High Road, in tunnel until just east of Gunnersbury station, whence it was proposed to secure running powers to Richmond and perhaps beyond. The Act received the Royal Assent on 15th August 1913, but the First World War changed the circumstances so much that the proposal was not revived in that form.

A few miles to the north, an act obtained by the Great Western Railway in 1905 enabled them to build a new double track line from their through station at Ealing Broadway, north east to North Acton to connect with their new High Wycombe line, then south east and east via East Acton to connect with the West London Line at Viaduct Junction, north of Shepherd's Bush. The new line, to be known as the Ealing & Shepherd's Bush Railway, included a short spur to a site bounded by Uxbridge Road, Caxton Road and Sterne Street, with subway connection to Shepherd's Bush Central London station. This spur was later curtailed, and instead the Central London obtained powers, on 18th August 1911, to extend their line from Wood Lane to join the ESB just north of Wood Lane station, then to Ealing Broadway by use of running powers. The realisation of this scheme will be described in the next chapter.

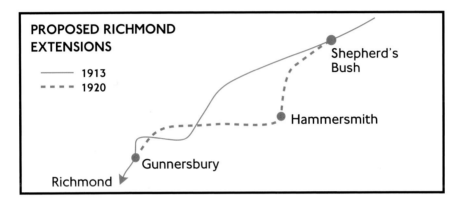

The Underground Group saw that the way to a profitable future lay in co-ordinated marketing, increased fares and the elimination of competition. By April 1912 it had purchased the London General Omnibus Company, and within twelve months had acquired or made agreements with all other London bus companies and two large tramway companies. Meanwhile, traffic on the Central London and the City & South London had continued to decline in the face of bus competition, and in late 1912 the Underground Group made offers for both companies. The holders of Central London ordinary stock would receive equal amounts of 4% guaranteed stock with a contingent right to 40% of higher earnings if earned for three successive years. Both groups of shareholders accepted, and both railways were formally taken over from 1st January 1913, although retaining their separate formal identities. At first the humble passengers had evidence of financial integration in relatively minor changes – standardised commercial advertisement sizes, bull's-eyes behind station nameplates, compressed air operation of lift gates, and a halfpenny reduction of the end to end fare. There were more through fares, including bookings from the tubes to trams and buses. The Underground Group management was convinced of the benefits of trains non-stopping certain intermediate stations, and this was soon applied to the Central London. From December 1913, Monday to Friday rush hour trains non-stopped Lancaster Gate, Queen's Road or Holland Park in rotation, thereby saving one minute on journeys to and from the central area. The outbreak of the First World War prevented more spectacular improvements to the Central London, but exciting developments were promised when peace returned.

Ealing and Other Adventures

In common with other railways, the Central London Railway suffered from worsening overcrowding and shortage of fuel and materials as the First World War wore on, but there was one beneficial effect, which arose indirectly. The District was the only one of the Underground Group lines to come under Government control, which meant that it was the only one that could pay war bonuses to the staff. The tube staff naturally thought that they, too, should have bonuses, and Albert Stanley obtained Board of Trade approval for a Common Fund. The participants were the District, the London Electric Railway, the CLR, the CSLR and the London General Omnibus Company. Each company would pay its surplus receipts into a pool each half year, after deducting certain agreed standing charges. The pool was then distributed in agreed proportions to the five companies. If any company could not meet its standing charges, the fund would make up the deficiency. The Central London portion of the fund, which was sanctioned by Act of Parliament and operated from 1st January 1915, was 20%. The practical effect was for the LGOC to subsidise the railways.

The Great Western Railway had completed the Ealing & Shepherd's Bush Railway for operation by steam hauled freight trains on 16th April 1917, but projection of Central London trains to Ealing could not be started until the end of hostilities. The line opened for passenger traffic on 3rd August 1920, after a directors' inspection and formal luncheon on 28th July. The basic weekday frequency was a train every 10 minutes.

A directors' inspection train headed by one of the 24 'Ealing motor cars' entering the unfinished Ealing Broadway terminal platform on 28th July 1920. A District train may be seen on the left. Ealing Libraries

Above **The special train has just stopped, and a group of railway officials and a press photographer await an important passenger.**
Ealing Libraries

Left **Lord George Hamilton alights. He had been chairman of the Central London from 1913 to 1919, and was to continue as Deputy Chairman until 1927, the year of his death.**
Ealing Libraries

Two extension tracks branched off the Wood Lane loop, one on each side, and immediately entered new subsurface platforms. The westbound platform (No.4) was curved and the eastbound (No.3) straight, and all four were connected to the Wood Lane ticket office and entrance by subways, stairways and a footbridge.

North of the station triangle, the two tracks ran close to one another, and were connected by a facing crossover. They continued on the east side of the Wood Lane thoroughfare, then swung westwards under the Wood Lane road overbridge, which was rebuilt at a higher level to allow enough clearance for the trains. Wood Lane Junction (so called, near Wormwood Scrubs prison) was the physical junction between the electric line and the main Ealing and Shepherd's Bush. The westbound Central London joined the westbound ESB line, which crossed over the eastbound Central London by a skew bridge to regain left hand running. The eastbound ESB and Central London split from each other just west of Wormwood Scrubs. Continuing to Ealing, the ESB was on embankment, passing East Acton station, then, after crossing below the Great Western main line, entered a cutting to run parallel to the Old Oak Common–High Wycombe line.

A North Acton station with platforms on both the ESB and the High Wycombe line was opened on 5th November 1923. A short distance further west was North Acton Junction, where connecting tracks allowed steam trains to run through between the eastern half of the ESB and High Wycombe. The ESB then turned south west, away from the 'new line'. It continued, mostly in cutting, past the future West Acton station (opened on the same day as North Acton) soon to enter the wide cutting used by the Great Western main line which was further widened, with retaining walls. This led to the terminus at Ealing Broadway, where a double track connection was provided with the GWR relief lines. A new island platform was built as a terminus for the Central London trains, squeezed in between the District terminus and the GWR up relief platform. There was also a connection to the District tracks, to permit rolling stock transfers.

The earthworks for the ESB were noteworthy in having the formation wide enough to allow the construction of two further tracks between Wood Lane and North Acton, and bridges allowing similar widening thence to Ealing Broadway. Some of the overbridges were of ferro-concrete, on the Hennibique system, but others were of steel girders,

The three intermediate stations were of the 'halt' type, with 300ft timber platforms outside the tracks, furnished with small shelters, and a small red brick ticket office at the road entrance. At Ealing Broadway, the platform was 640ft long and was equipped with Great Western standard verandah roofing, mounted centrally; a new footbridge, at the east end of the station, connected the platforms of all three railways. Track was to GWR standard, of 97^1/$_2$lb per yard bull head rails, on hardwood sleepers and slag ballast. The central positive conductor rail was installed, and at stations the ballast was made up to give a 1ft 8in platform height for the tube trains.

The extension added 4.33 miles to those served by Central London trains; 4.18 miles were owned by the Great Western, the rest being the short links north of Wood Lane station. The Great Western had installed three-position upper quadrant semaphore signals at Paddington in 1914, and used them throughout the ESB. New or enlarged signalboxes were at Wood Lane station, Wood Lane Junction, North Acton and Ealing Broadway. Electrical power came from the Great Western's station at Park Royal, via Old Oak Common substation. This power station closed in 1936, with the new source of energy being the Metropolitan Electric Supply Co.

Two views of a Brush built motor car, one of 24 ordered for the Ealing extension and one of 22 loaned initially to the Bakerloo for its extension to Watford in 1917. The track for the Ealing extension was completed in the same year but start of passenger service was delayed by the First World War.

In 1912 the Central London ordered 24 new motor cars for the Ealing extension from the Brush company. Twenty two of these were delivered by 1917, to be commandeered for the Bakerloo extension to Watford Junction; they were brought back to their intended line as soon as new Joint Tube Stock for the Watford line had been delivered and the temporary fourth rail current collectors had been removed from the Brush cars' motor bogies. The Central London gained from the short migration by having more substantial motor bogies fitted to the stock. The original equaliser bar bogies had not stood up to high speed running, and were replaced by Cammell Laird plate-frame and angle bogies whilst working on the Bakerloo.

The 24 cars introduced some new features for tube rolling stock. They were the first all-enclosed tube cars, and the first to have automatic acceleration, with the electro-magnetic contactors being controlled by a current limit relay. There were swing doors on each side, at the ends as well as just behind the equipment compartment. They had arch roofs over the whole car, and seats for 32, of which eight were transverse. Twenty-four trailers and 24 control trailers were modified for the Ealing service by having heaters fitted, and side extensions to the clerestory projections over the platforms (22 of the control trailers had been so modified in 1915 and stored). The 72 cars were known as the 'Ealing stock', and had to be kept separate from the other cars (now known as 'Tunnel stock') because of the technical differences. As the Ealing traffic increased, more stock suitable for open air running was needed, and eight 'tunnel' motor coaches were similarly converted (including more powerful 240hp motors and automatic acceleration) in 1925-26, together with eight trailers which were concurrently converted to control trailers.

Much of the Ealing extension was at first through open country, and traffic was depressed by having to charge the higher Great Western fares. Agreement was reached to lower these to Underground levels from 1st May 1922, and traffic increased with the development of housing and factory estates.

During the war, the London and South Western Railway service between Kensington, Shepherd's Bush and Richmond was withdrawn, and in 1920 powers were obtained to link the Central London into this line at Shepherd's Bush. In 1913 the Underground Group had also gained powers to extend the Piccadilly Line from Hammersmith over the LSWR tracks to Richmond, and this scheme (as later modified) eventually proved to have more attractions than that of the Central.

The Underground Group had long been concerned about the cost of employing the numerous gatemen on tube stock with end gates, and the delays at stations caused by passengers moving through the narrow end doors and car platforms. In 1919 forty new trailers with sliding doors were ordered for the Piccadilly Line, to be marshalled with 20 motor cars of 1906 vintage which had been sent away for sliding air-operated doors to be fitted. This programme was not completed until December 1923.

At that time gate stock cars with steel bodies were working on the Bakerloo and Hampstead lines, but on the Central London most of the gate stock had wooden bodies. In 1924 two trailers were selected for experimental conversion, one from the Central and one from the Hampstead. Adapting the steel bodied Hampstead car with door openings in the sides (and pockets for the doors to slide into) proved very expensive, and after a few more experiments the conclusion was reached that it would be more economical to scrap the steel cars and buy modern ones (later known as 'standard stock') to replace them.

The Central London experiment was more successful. The end platforms were enclosed, the internal bulkheads removed, and the space provided with passenger seats and windows (or an enclosed cab on control trailers). Two single leaf sliding doors were fitted in the trailer sides, about one third and two thirds of the distance along the body. Fitting standard double doors was not practical because it would have needed extensive body strengthening. Compared with the two 4ft 6in door openings of the standard stock trailers being built in the 1920s, the two 3ft 3in openings for the shorter Central London cars were not unreasonably narrow.

The single car was run as part of a gate stock train in 1925, with the gateman opening the doors by end air cocks. No important drawbacks were found, and it was decided to convert the whole fleet of 259 cars. On the motor cars, there was one intermediate passenger doorway with two sliding doors, and a swing door for the guard at the trailing end. A similar swing door was fitted on the control trailer cabs.

The conversion was undertaken by the Union Construction Company at Feltham, a hitherto dormant Underground Group subsidiary. It involved a great deal of woodwork and seat rearrangement, with new vestibules flanking the new door openings, but the scheme had the advantage that the cars retained their original overall dimensions. There were numerous irregularities and misalignments in the Central London tunnels, which would have had to be expensively rectified to accommodate standard stock (as had to be done in 1938-9) and it was felt that the balance of advantage lay with the conversion scheme. The first whole train converted to air doors ran in September 1926, and the last entered service in 1928. In order to relieve any shortage of stock while the cars were away at Feltham, two air-doored trains were borrowed from the Piccadilly Line, and equipped with smaller wheels to allow for the Central's reduced clearances.

Central London cars in the Union Construction Company's Feltham Works at various stages of reconstruction. Apart from one experimental conversion, work started on 1st March 1926.

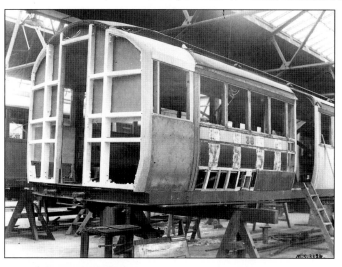

Left **Heavy reconstruction was needed, with complete new car ends, new door openings and vestibules, renewed framing and new panels.**

Below **With its sliding doors and the former end platform enclosed, a trailer car is ready to move back to Wood Lane depot for another 13 years' work.**

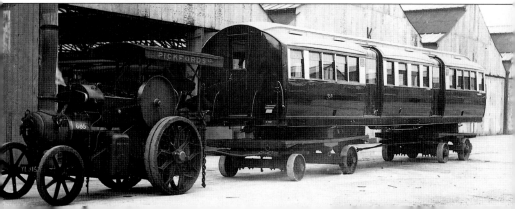

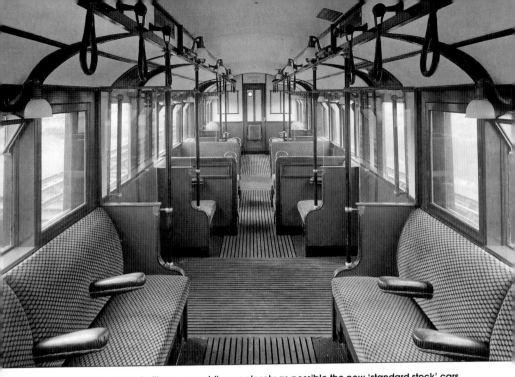

The interior of a rebuilt car, resembling as closely as possible the new 'standard stock' cars of the same period.

An air-doored 1903 motor car heads a train on the last stage of its journey to Ealing Broadway.

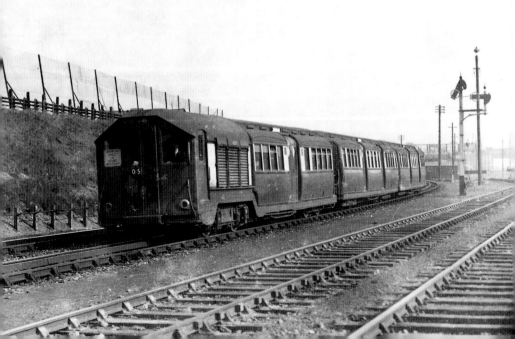

At first two guards were required on an air-doored six-car train, but after the development of a driver/guard telephone loudspeaker system it was possible to use only one. After a successful experiment in August 1927, the telephone system was fitted at Wood Lane depot (except for a few cars modified at Feltham); all trains were equipped by July 1928.

A further step was achieved in the integration of the Central London into the Underground Group when it began to take its power supply from Lots Road power station on 18th March 1928 and the Wood Lane power station was closed. The CLR rotary converters at substations were adapted from 25 cycles per second to the Underground standard of $33^1/3$. The changeover also involved laying high tension cables between Lots Road and a newly-equipped substation at Wood Lane, closing Post Office substation, and taking feeds from Russell Square via a switch house at Holborn and from Mansion House via a switch house at Bank.

Another step towards integration was demonstrated in rebuilding stations to the standards of new stations elsewhere on the Underground. Between 1924 and 1934, escalators replaced lifts at Shepherd's Bush, Bond Street, Marble Arch, Oxford Circus, Tottenham Court Road, Chancery Lane and Bank. In addition improved interchange was constructed at those stations also served by other tube lines.

Bond Street was converted to an escalator-equipped station in 1926, and the frontage was an early example of Charles Holden's work for the Underground. LT Museum

In 1927 greyhound racing began at White City stadium, and passenger flows at Wood Lane increased greatly. The old large ticket office in the circulating area was demolished and replaced by smaller island type offices. With the old gate stock, the end platforms were close to the platform edge when the outside platform (No.2) was used. Rebuilt stock with intermediate doors had a smaller gap when it used platform No.1 on the inside of the curve. Therefore movement was concentrated on this platform, and an extra footbridge built for incoming passengers. The existing footbridge to the ticket hall was used by outgoing passengers. No.1 platform had to be extended to take 6-car trains, but as the extension fouled the entry track from the depot, it consisted of a section of movable platform. This could swing back to allow exit from the depot; its movement was interlocked with the signalling from the Wood Lane box; it was installed in March 1928.

Wood Lane platform 1, on the inside of the loop. The station opened in May 1908, and the movable section of platform in March 1928. Of the tracks visible beyond the platform, the nearer leads from the depot and the other from Shepherd's Bush. LT Museum

One of the brand-new Holborn platforms in November 1933, where the 1903 motor car looks anachronistic. LT Museum

The 170yd-long street interchange between British Museum and Holborn (Piccadilly Line) stations had long been a weak point in the Underground network, and there had been proposals for a low level subway as early as 1907. In 1914 parliamentary powers were obtained to move British Museum station eastwards to Holborn, but no work was done because of the outbreak of war. With Government financial assistance announced in 1929, work could be resumed. New powers were obtained in 1930, and contracts were let in October of that year. The scheme involved the reconstruction and enlargement of Holborn ticket hall, and the construction of a four-escalator shaft to an intermediate landing, subsequently equipped with four machines. New Central London platforms were built in station tunnels constructed round the running tunnels, which were later dismantled. These platforms were on the outside of the tracks, as there was no spare space between the running tunnels. On 22nd May 1933 the station was renamed Holborn (Kingsway), and work on the combined station was completed on 25th September. British Museum had closed the previous day and its siding was signalled from a new 11-lever frame at the west end of the westbound Central platform at Holborn. By 1938 the volume of interchange traffic was ten times that of the former interchange at street level.

Despite this record of improvement, there was a great deal of public dissatisfaction with the scale of public transport being provided under the competitive system, and ideas for a common financial fund and common management for underground railways, buses and trams were put forward by Lord Ashfield and Frank Pick, heads of the Underground Group. After a Labour Government came to power in 1929 a London Passenger Transport Bill was introduced. This survived the fall of Labour in 1931, and became law on 13th April 1933. The new London Passenger Transport Board began to operate on 1st July 1933, and the Central London Railway ceased to have an effective separate existence, although it was not legally wound up until 10th March 1939.

The Early London Transport Years

In east London the inadequacy of the steam hauled passenger service along the Romford–Ilford–Stratford–Liverpool Street axis had long been notorious, and the impecunious London & North Eastern Railway had periodically commissioned electrification studies, regretfully concluding that the cost was more than it could bear. For a change, a tube railway between Ilford and Liverpool Street was studied in 1930, but the cost (£7^1/$_2$ million) was deemed too great because most of the traffic was concentrated in the peak hours. The local railway users' association wanted a Central London extension to Eastern Avenue (where much speculative housing development had taken place) and on to Romford, with a branch to Barkingside and Claybury. The LNER reverted to the concept of straightforward electrification on the overhead wire system, comprising the lines down to Gidea Park or Shenfield, round the Fairlop loop to Woodford, and over the Loughton branch right out to Ongar. This was considered by the joint main line/London Transport traffic committee in conjunction with a Central London extension to Goodmayes (Little Heath) via Mile End and North Ilford. The large proportion of peak traffic and the high costs of construction indicated that both schemes would be permanent loss makers. Government would not agree a subsidy, and the LNER stuck obstinately to its own scheme. Adjudication resolved the impasse by diverting the Central London extension to Newbury Park, and then grafting on the Fairlop loop to Woodford and the Ongar branch as far as Loughton. The LNER was left with overhead electrification of the Liverpool Street–Shenfield line, and the future of the Loughton–Ongar section was temporarily left in limbo.

This plan for huge Central London extensions in the east was accompanied by a planned western extension from North Acton to Ruislip parallel to the High Wycombe line, and extensive physical improvements to the original line to make it conform more closely to Underground Group standards.

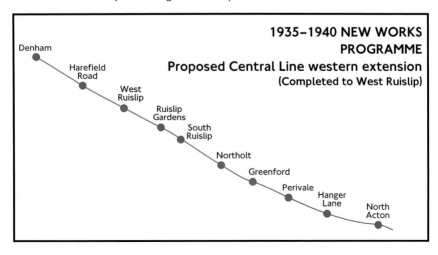

1935–1940 NEW WORKS PROGRAMME
Proposed Central Line western extension
(Completed to West Ruislip)

Denham
Harefield Road
West Ruislip
Ruislip Gardens
South Ruislip
Northolt
Greenford
Perivale
Hanger Lane
North Acton

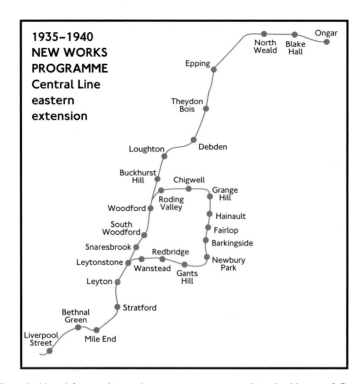

1935–1940 NEW WORKS PROGRAMME Central Line eastern extension

Ongar
North Weald
Blake Hall
Epping
Theydon Bois
Loughton
Debden
Buckhurst Hill
Chigwell
Grange Hill
Roding Valley
Woodford
Hainault
South Woodford
Fairlop
Snaresbrook
Barkingside
Redbridge
Newbury Park
Leytonstone
Wanstead
Leyton
Gants Hill
Stratford
Bethnal Green
Liverpool Street
Mile End

These bold and far-reaching schemes were announced to the House of Commons on 5th and 18th June 1935. Together with schemes to improve the Bakerloo, Metropolitan and what became the Northern Line, and to rebuild many stations, they were known collectively as the 1935-40 New Works Programme. Government support came in the form of guarantees of interest on loans, which enabled finance to be raised at a lower rate of interest than would have been available by a direct approach to the market (2$\frac{1}{2}$% instead of about 3$\frac{3}{4}$%).

The line from Stratford to Loughton had been opened in 1856 by the Eastern Counties Railway, which became part of the Great Eastern Railway in 1862. There were stations at Low Leyton (just 'Leyton' from 1867), Leytonstone, Snaresbrook, George Lane (now South Woodford), Woodford, Buckhurst Hill and Loughton (with a terminus near the High Street). This double track line had a single track extension from a junction south of Loughton to Ongar in 1865, which had been doubled as far as Epping by 1893. Stations were provided at Chigwell Road (later renamed Chigwell Lane, and subsequently Debden), Theydon (Theydon Bois in late 1865), Epping, North Weald, Blake Hall and Ongar. The Fairlop loop had been an unwise 20th century (1903) venture by the Great Eastern. It left the Shenfield main line by a triangular junction just east of Ilford, and looped round via Hainault to terminate on the Ongar branch at Woodford. Intermediate stations were provided at Newbury Park, Barkingside, Fairlop, Hainault, Grange Hill, and Chigwell. Roding Valley was added in 1936. Built solidly with handsome closely-spaced stations, it failed to encourage the building development that would have generated enough traffic to make the venture worth while.

The experience gained from many years of building Underground railways was used to good effect in the Central London extensions, with such desirable features as cross-platform interchanges with other lines and new stations at road intersections where they could feed a network of bus services.

On leaving Liverpool Street, the extension, in twin tube tunnels, swung north east to serve Bethnal Green, then south east to Mile End for cross-platform interchange with the District Line. Again turning north east to run below the Great Eastern main line, it briefly came to the surface at a rebuilt and resited Stratford station to give cross-platform interchange with the Shenfield line stopping services. Leaving Stratford, the separate Central London tracks re-entered tunnel to swing north below the main line tracks and surface again south of Leyton to join the Ongar branch at a flat surface junction. Immediately north of Leytonstone, one track branched off on each side and dived down to the new Eastern Avenue tube, with intermediate stations at Wanstead, Redbridge and Gants Hill. Then there was another change of direction as the tunnels swung first south east and then north to break surface on each side of the Fairlop loop just south of Newbury Park. The Central London would then take over the loop passenger service to Hainault and on to Woodford.

In west London a new pair of electrified tracks was to be built, parallel to and south of the GWR/GCR High Wycombe line, opened between 1903 and 1906. The new extension ran from a junction with the Ealing and Shepherd's Bush line, about half a mile west of North Acton station, to Ruislip & Ickenham (renamed West Ruislip in 1947), just beyond a new depot.

Most parts of the 1935 programme which needed parliamentary powers were approved in the LPTB, GWR and LNER Acts of 1936, including the all-important repeal of the clause in the Central London's 1909 Act which had forbidden a tube extension beyond Liverpool Street. In 1936, it was intended that the new open-air sections, although served by Central London trains, would remain as part of the GWR or LNER, and these railways were responsible for construction work on new tracks, part of the electrification work, and for stations and other buildings. However, the LPTB kept control of all the signalling installations.

Some additions to the 1935 plan were made in the following years. In 1937 two extra electric tracks were authorised between Ruislip and Denham, and station reconstruction at Liverpool Street and Notting Hill Gate; London Transport also proposed to extend the electrification from Loughton to Ongar and to secure the provision of two new tracks between Wood Lane Junction and North Acton solely for Great Western goods traffic. In recognition of the lengthy extensions into Essex and Middlesex the Central London Line became merely the 'Central Line' from 28th August 1937. In 1938 a new station at Wood Lane and an extra interchange subway at Tottenham Court Road were approved.

As mentioned earlier, the Central Line tunnels, although nominally of 11ft 8¼in internal diameter (except for 11ft 6in just outside stations), had been built to less exacting standards than later tube lines; some of the lining segments were up to 8in out of true alignment. Better alignments were needed, not only to allow the passage of trains of standard tube dimensions, but also to allow higher running speeds and to give clearance for the installation of a second current rail to convert the Central to the Underground four-rail standard. There was also the continuing task of converting from bridge rails to bull head rail with cross timbers, of which only one third had been completed. Finally, a decision had to be made on the related questions of platform lengths and the type of rolling stock to replace the museum pieces of 1900.

Realigning the running tunnels to take standard rolling stock. The top segment is removed by special jack, then segments which are out of alignment are removed and sent to Wood Lane depot for regrinding. Surplus clay is skimmed off and the ring re-assembled with reground segments and packing pieces to increase the diameter, May 1937. LT Museum

When the 1935-40 New Works Programme was being prepared, the Morden–Edgware line had a severe overcrowding problem, but future overcrowding could also be expected on the central sections of the Bakerloo and Central London lines when the proposed extensions had been completed, so there were three lines needing relief. At first there were thoughts of buying new standard stock for the Northern City and Bakerloo lines and a whole new fleet for the Central London. Meanwhile the rolling stock engineers had been busy exploring how to increase passenger accommodation by squeezing equipment beneath the car floor and using smaller traction motors, resulting in the experimental 1935 stock. With new rolling stock of this type and improved signalling, it would be possible to increase the Morden–Edgware line capacity by 25%, and so avoid the expense of lengthening 90 platforms on that line to take longer trains. So the decision was taken to equip the Morden–Edgware line entirely with new stock; to use similar stock on about half the Bakerloo workings and lengthen its 30 tube platforms to take seven-car trains; and to equip the Central London with 'standard stock' (1923-1927) from the other lines and lengthen its 26 tube platforms from 325 to 427ft to accommodate eight-car trains. The tunnel realignment was done by gangs who came each night on a train of service wagons, hauled from Wood Lane depot by a battery locomotive. Segments were removed and the grout and clay behind skimmed with pneumatic tools. The segments were replaced and regrouted, and any displaced cables reinstated. Station lengthening was achieved by building a length of station tunnel round the running tunnel, which was then demolished. However, the 'hump' construction of station platforms caused some problems, as there was a Ministry of Transport recommendation that platforms should not have a steeper slope than 1 in 264. Therefore the track and running tunnel beyond the extended platform had to be raised to meet the end of the extension. Usually the extension was made at the approach side of the station, where the gradient was 1 in 60, rather than the departure side, with its 1 in 30. By taking advantage of the permitted slope in the platform extension, it was usually possible to limit the distance for which the running line and roof of the running tunnel had to be raised to about 80ft. There was a problem at Shepherd's Bush, where the western ends of the platforms were fixed by staircases and the eastern ends by converging running lines.

Fortunately some space was available in a disused crossover tunnel. This was enlarged to move the running tracks apart, and an island platform extension built between them. Extension at Liverpool Street, with its crossover tunnels at each end, also needed some delicate work. At its east end, the dead-end siding tunnels were extended as reversing tunnels between the running tunnels.

Work proceeded concurrently on replacement of the remaining ten miles of bridge type running rail and the installation of positive conductor rail outside the running rails. As clearances were still tight, this had to be installed 4^1/$_2$in above the running rails instead of the standard 3in, and, additionally, special 'L' section conductor rail had to be fitted in many places. Consequently trains needed modified positive shoegear.

With the realignment work completed, there was a gauging run by standard stock on the night of 12th November 1938, and the first passenger-carrying train of such stock ran on 15th November. These trains had been passed through Acton Works for overhaul, modernisation, and temporary modification of current collection so that the centre shoes became positive and the other pole was connected to earth return. The flow of standard stock released from the Northern Line by new 1938 stock enabled all the old Central London cars to be withdrawn. The last normal passenger train of old stock ran on 10th June 1939, and there was a formal last day on 12th July. The sole remaining electric locomotive at Wood Lane was withdrawn at the same time, and scrapped in 1942. Finally the four-rail system came into use on the night of 4th/5th May 1940. This removal of return traction current from the running rails enabled standard LT type signalling to be commissioned. The line was wholly resignalled to allow a more frequent and speedier train service. Signal boxes were retained at the reversing points of Queen's Road and Marble Arch; Holborn had had a new box for the British Museum siding in 1933, and there was another new box at Liverpool Street. Bank box was kept but Shepherd's Bush, Wood Lane Junction and North Acton boxes closed in 1938.

The Twopenny Tube

To those who, in the words of the Silurist, "by backward steps would move," a piece of news in this journal yesterday offered a rich chance of comfortable and philosophic sadness. The last train of the old type left on the Central London Line had been taken on its last journey. The poor old thing is out of date, a back number, a dug-out. It might be a Harrovian, so deep have forty—to be precise, thirty-nine—years plunged it into senile decay. Thirty-nine years ago it seemed incredibly smart, swift, and luxurious. It was driven by electricity, not steam; and those who knew what atmosphere the smoke could make in the Inner Circle stations of Portland Road and Gower Street (which the lust of change has renamed Great Portland Street and Euston Road) rejoiced at the clearness of the air in the stations of the new line. The carriages were generously lit by electricity; one could read in them with ease. They were not cut up into compartments, each with a door which none could open from outside if some curmudgeonly passenger inside chose to put his foot against the handle. And spacious lifts " descend to meet every train "—which was better than stairs, although *Punch* soon found occasion to amend the notice into " condescend to meet some trains."

How simple, too, the booking ! Every fare was the same. For twopence the passenger might travel from terminus to terminus of the railway, which Cockney wit promptly named the " Twopenny Tube "—from Shepherd's Bush to the Bank. From Shepherd's Bush to Holland Park, or from the Post Office to the Bank was also a twopenny fare. The passenger put down his twopence, took his ticket and dropped it into a box at the barrier; and that was that. The company soon found cause to graduate the fares and to replace the box by a human ticket-collector; but the early days of nonchalance are still treasured in the memory of those who knew them. And now all that was so new and so grand in 1900 is falling fast under the sickle of the Reaper. The old trains are museum pieces, like the hansom and the horse bus; and the noble and condescending lift is rapidly being ousted in favour of the moving staircase—the escalator, which the Portland Place authority on English pronunciation has more than once rhymed with Ballater.

Facing page **Replacing the old bridge rails on longitudinal timbers by bull-head rail. Marble Arch, May 1938.** LT Museum

Left **The last appearance on the Central Line of the original Central London Railway rolling stock was commemorated in a Times editorial on 14th July 1939, two days after the formal last day of use. The trains, substantially rebuilt in 1926-28, had managed almost forty years' service.** Capital Transport collection

As the most important Central Line stations in the central area had already been rebuilt, there was not much further work on stations in the 1935-40 period. However, in May 1937 Tottenham Court Road had a new relief subway parallel to the westbound Central Line platform, and a deep level subway between the Central and Northern Lines was opened in November 1939.

Post Office station had the most far-reaching changes. In October 1935 a start was made in excavating a new ticket hall beneath Newgate Street, Cheapside and St Martins le Grand, and the station was renamed St Paul's (Post Office) on 1st February 1937. The new ticket hall was opened on 1st January 1939, with three escalators down to westbound platform level (one of which was soon commandeered for war service and never replaced) and two more, flanking fixed stairs, to the eastbound platform. Five lifts were superseded, and the street ticket office at King Edward Street/Newgate Street was closed.

The extension work made a promising start. The most difficult section, from Mile End to Leyton, was begun first, in October 1936. Here, water-bearing soil made work expensive and difficult. The Liverpool Street–Mile End contract was awarded in March 1937, and that for the new Hainault depot in August. Other major contracts followed swiftly, the last one for new tunnels being awarded in August 1938. Eastwards from Liverpool Street to just west of Mile End, rotary excavators and shields cut through blue clay.

Further east, in the Lea Valley marshes, the soil was saturated with water, and much work had to be done in compressed air. Chemical soil consolidation was also employed, especially where there was a risk that compressed air alone might blow out the thin layer of subsoil above the new tunnel. Notable applications of this technique included injecting the chemical mixture into the bed of the City Mill river from pipes beneath pontoons, and into the subsoil below and around the LNER Loughton Branch Junction signalbox, where only four feet separated the top of a tunnel from the box foundations.

From just east of Fairfield Road, Bow to Stratford the new tube was beneath the LNER embankment, and encountered difficulties passing under the branches of the River Lea and adjacent abutments of railway bridges. At such points, driving the new tunnels called for very high degrees of ingenuity in design and skill in execution, which were also demanded north of Stratford, where there could be no question of suspending the main line services to allow construction of the covered ways for the tube beneath.

At Mile End the Central Line used the outsides of the existing District platforms. An existing open cutting gave space on the south side, but on the north side the retaining wall was demolished, a trench dug, and a new mass concrete wall built below the roadway. The pre-war rearmament programme caused a shortage of steel. Tests at Wood Lane confirmed that concrete segments had adequate strength to resist pressure from above and from the thrust of advancing tunnelling shields. They were two inches thick compared with seven-eighths of an inch for cast iron, and had bolt holes reinforced with steel for bolting to their neighbours. They were used for $2^3/4$ miles of running tunnel east of Gants Hill, and gave a tunnel of 12ft 3in internal diameter. This 3in increase over the standard tunnel size for new construction was to allow space for signal apparatus, as the concrete flanges had less space between them than the iron ones. To speed up the tunnelling work, large numbers of Greathead shields and rotary excavators were used at once, and at one stage 40 different sections of tunnel were being built simultaneously,

Newly completed subway entrance at Gants Hill shortly after the start of the 1939-45 war. Opening of the station was delayed until 1947.
LT Museum

At Redbridge the original plan was for the new line to cross the River Roding by bridge, but this was replaced by cut and cover work, with reinforced concrete tunnels of rectangular shape. Redbridge station is so shallow that access can be gained by a short staircase. Here again, water bearing strata were encountered, and the work had to be done under compressed air, with the consequent need to pass men and materials through air locks. It was one of a number of stations to have had various names suggested for it between the announcement of the New Works Programme in 1935 and its opening. 'Red House' was an early suggestion, as was 'Ilford West'. Neighbouring Gants Hill had alternative suggestions 'Cranbrook' and 'Ilford North', one committee meeting noting that Gants Hill, as a name, was not liked.

The Stratford–Ongar line closely followed the land contours, and was therefore plagued by numerous level crossings. In 1936 Parliament had ruled that six level crossings of public roads should be replaced by underpasses or overbridges before electric trains could run. These were at the junction of Grove Green Road and Church Lane, Leytonstone; Eagle Lane, Wanstead; George Lane, South Woodford; Snakes Lane, Woodford; Queens Road, Buckhurst Hill; and Coppice Row, Theydon Bois. Delays arose from having to rely on other authorities, and from legal technicalities, and in 1939 the LPTB obtained powers to seek permission of the Minister of Transport to close level crossings if the new crossings were not complete but the railway was otherwise ready. After the war, permission was given to permanently sever the road connections at Eagle Lane, Wanstead and Queens Road, Buckhurst Hill. In the case of the latter an east-west road connection already existed about 200 yards north of Queens Road. At Grove Green Road/Church Lane, Leytonstone, the junction was moved and Church Lane extended to cross under the railway. At George Lane, motor traffic was directed via a new road around South Woodford station. At Snakes Lane a new east-west road connection was provided a quarter of a mile to the south by the extension of Broadmead Road to meet Chigwell Road. A new overbridge replaced the level crossing at Theydon Bois. Pedestrian rights of way on the extension were maintained by subways or footbridges.

In west London the Great Western Railway started building the two extra tracks from North Acton to Ruislip. These involved the widenings of cuttings and embankments and the construction or lengthening of numerous bridges. Work began at the North Acton end, and double track was laid as far as Greenford by outbreak of war. The extra freight tracks between Wood Lane Junction and North Acton were opened to traffic on 19th June 1938, concurrently with the closure to freight trains of Ealing Broadway–North Acton. Henceforth the Central Line trains no longer had to share their tracks with Great Western milk trains bound for Shepherd's Bush depot.

The Central Line on War Service

In August 1937 it had been expected that the extension to Greenford would open in January 1940, to West Ruislip in July, and to Denham in March 1941. For the eastern extensions, a Commons question in March 1940 produced the following estimates – Loughton by the end of 1940; Newbury Park and the Hainault loop by early 1941. The outbreak of war in September 1939 had initially caused thoughts of stopping all New Works Programme work immediately, but in November 1939 the Board and the main lines agreed to try to complete the Central Line extensions to Greenford and Loughton, but to postpone the station improvements at Notting Hill Gate and Liverpool Street. The new Loughton station was opened to LNER trains on 28th April 1940, but the war situation deteriorated so quickly that new tracklaying was suspended from 24th May, and all other work by June 1940, except for works which were so advanced that it would be dangerous to leave them unfinished.

As soon as London's aerial bombardment began, all vacant tunnels were examined as prospective air raid shelters. In the unfinished Central Line tunnels nearest to central London, tracks had been laid in the eastbound bore from the Leyton portal to about one third of a mile east of Liverpool Street, but in the westbound only as far as Mile End. The incomplete Bethnal Green station had been used as a shelter for the first three nights of heavy bombing, but was then closed by London Transport because of the danger of flooding. After a tour by Mr (later Sir) Herbert Morrison, Minister of Home Security, on 5th October 1940, permission was given for the use of the station and about a mile of tunnel towards Liverpool Street; the unopened sidings east of Liverpool Street were also used for shelterers, as were short sections of unopened tunnel at Leytonstone, Leyton and Stratford.

Further east, about 2½ route miles of twin tube tunnel between Whipps Cross and just east of Gants Hill were made over to the Plessey Company for a military components factory, with 300,000 sq ft of floor space, and employing 2,000 workers in shifts covering the 24 hours. A false floor was installed, with air conditioning ducts below and 9ft 3in headroom to the apex of the tube tunnel. There was an 18in gauge railway in each bore to transport materials by battery locomotives. Workers gained access via the unfinished Gants Hill, Redbridge and Wanstead stations, but additional access points were provided by sinking shafts at Cambridge Park and Danehurst Gardens and equipping them with lifts. Gants Hill and Wanstead both had at least one escalator working. Work on this project started late in 1940 and was completed in March 1942. Products included wiring sets for Halifax and Lancaster bombers, wireless equipment, cartridge starters for fighters, gear levers for armoured vehicles, shell fuses and field telephones. Some of the spoil from making the Deep Shelters nearer central London was deposited above the tunnels near Redbridge to increase the depth of cover, and floodgates were installed in the tunnel on each side of the crossing beneath the River Roding.

A war-scarred station in war-torn surroundings. The area around St Paul's suffered badly in the 1940 Blitz on London. LT Museum

Tube stations in use were also occupied by shelterers, as was the disused station at British Museum. Amenities for shelterers improved gradually, and the Central Line had the first 'tube refreshments special' train, on 6th November 1940. This ran daily in the midday period, and offloaded boxed food at each shelter station.

Although the deep level tube stations were relatively safe, and certainly quiet and dry compared with the battle raging above, they were not immune from bombs which penetrated weak points. One such bomb fell on Bank station at 8.00pm on 11th January 1941. It cut through the concourse just below the street and exploded in the escalator machine room. The Central Line escalators were completely wrecked, and the blast damaged two trains at the platforms 62ft below. 56 people were killed and 69 injured. As the roof of the concourse collapsed, there was a crater 120ft long by 100ft wide in the roadway. The army and civil defence workers made heroic efforts to clear the shambles, but the station was at first accessed by an open staircase, and a military type bridge was built for road traffic to cross the cavity. The roadway was partly reinstated by May 1941 and the bridge removed. One escalator (intended for Highgate) was installed by December 1941, and a second (borrowed from Chancery Lane) by April 1944.

The worst individual disaster at a tube station occurred at the unopened Bethnal Green just before 8.30pm on 3rd March 1943, on the poorly lit rough concrete stairway from the street. There had been an alert at 8.17, and people began pouring into the shelter, initially in a hurried but orderly way. At 8.27 a salvo of anti-aircraft rockets was fired about one-third of a mile away. The crowd entering the station surged forward, and a woman with a child tripped and fell near the foot of the staircase. Others fell over, but those entering pushed harder and fell in their turn on top of those in front, causing a large number of fatalities. It was found that 173 had died from suffocation and 62 had been injured. Swift measures were taken to build canopies around tube station and other shelter entrances so that stronger lighting could be installed, and to install central barriers down stairways and crush barriers at the top.

Building a platform-edge wall at the disused British Museum station in June 1941. The wall was publicised as allowing twice the number of bunks to be accommodated. A false floor has been added previously. A standard stock train passes en route for Liverpool Street.
LT Museum

Above **What was left of the Bank ticket hall on 14th January 1941, after a high explosive bomb had exploded in the escalator machine room on 11th January, killing 56 people and injuring 69. In the right background is St Mary Woolnoth church, beneath which the City & South London Railway excavated a ticket hall for its Bank station.** LT Museum

Left **Installing machines for the Plessey underground factory on Redbridge station platform in July 1941.** LT Museum

The effects of war were quickly apparent to the regular tube traveller. Apart from bomb damage to stations and sections of line (which were sometimes taken out of service for weeks at a time) there was the yellow protective netting on the windows, blackout train lighting on open sections of line, reduced train and station lighting to save fuel, stationary 'down' escalators at some stations, increased traffic and reduced services.

From the outbreak of war, all of London Transport's services, and those of the four main line railways and a few specified independent railways, had come under government control. Liaison between the railways and implementation of government instructions were undertaken by the Railway Executive Committee. Appointed on 24th September 1938, this consisted of senior representatives of the five undertakings. The REC did a vast amount of essential work in furthering the war effort, assisted by sixteen functional sub-committees. London Transport continued under REC control after the war ended, when most of the long delayed plans for the Central Line were finally realised.

The New Works Programme Resumed

With the end of hostilities, attention turned to resuming the New Works Programme from the points at which it had been suspended in 1939 and 1940. At first London Transport announced its intention to complete virtually all of the outstanding works, but its wartime optimism faced the realities of post-war shortages of labour and materials of all kinds (steel in particular) and, a little later, of changed traffic flows engendered by new and more effective town planning legislation.

However, the inadequacy of the steam hauled passenger services to Liverpool Street remained, and threatened to grow worse as employment in central London reverted to pre-war levels. The Minister of War Transport conveyed to the LPTB and the LNER the Cabinet's request that the highest priority be given to resuming work on the Central Line eastern and western extensions and the LNER overhead electrification from Liverpool Street to Shenfield.

There were many difficulties to resolve. As well as the general shortages of resources, the Central Line had its own share of special problems. Wartime works had to be removed (demolishing the Plessey tunnel factory took five months to remove the plant, and another seven to demolish the concrete floors, air conditioning and other infrastructure), the cramped Wood Lane depot could not be relieved until electrification reached the new depots at Hainault and Ruislip, trains could not be lengthened until Wood Lane station was replaced, much of the intended rolling stock had to be given an extra heavy overhaul because of open-air storage of much of it throughout the war, and the Epping line level crossing replacement programme had to be completed.

The extension programme began with the formal opening of the 4¼ mile Liverpool Street–Stratford section on 3rd December 1946 by the Minister of Transport, Alfred Barnes, with public service beginning the following day. The trains continued empty beyond Stratford, through the tunnels under the main LNER tracks, to reverse over an automatically-operated crossover just beyond the tunnel mouths. The first intermediate station, Bethnal Green, at the junction of Roman Road and Cambridge Heath Road, was of typical tube construction, with a 420ft station tunnel for each direction, linked by a concourse at one end, from which three escalators rose to the sub-surface ticket hall. There was a crossover just west of the station. Mile End was entirely different. As described earlier, the tubes rose to subsurface level to give cross-platform interchange with the District Line. The surface station was completely rebuilt in the flat Portland stone style based on Holden's designs of the early 1930s, whilst the platforms were obstructed by numerous pillars, giving a rather gloomy effect overall. Both tube lines rose to the open air at Stratford, giving cross-platform interchange to the LNER local services. Below platform level, stairs and short subways gave access to a concourse which was handy for the platforms on the North Woolwich line, but a long walk from the main ticket office via a subterranean subway. The tube platforms were equipped with modern waiting rooms and a snack bar on the eastbound side. Tube services were every four minutes (peak) and every five minutes (off peak).

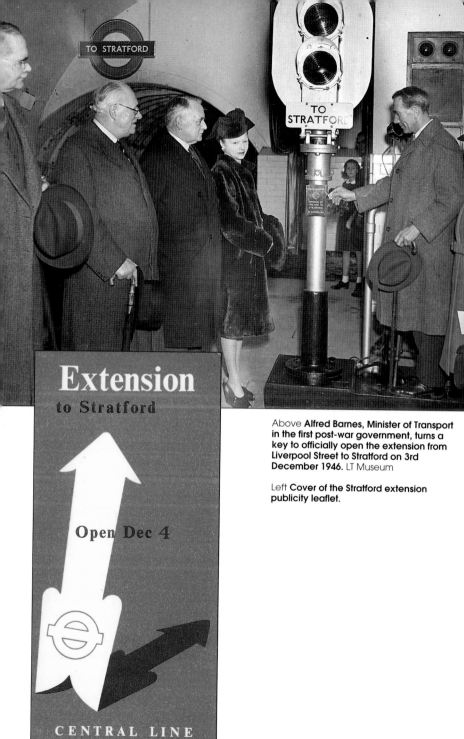

Extension
to Stratford

Open Dec 4

CENTRAL LINE

Above **Alfred Barnes, Minister of Transport in the first post-war government, turns a key to officially open the extension from Liverpool Street to Stratford on 3rd December 1946.** LT Museum

Left **Cover of the Stratford extension publicity leaflet.**

Above **Work in hand to adapt Leytonstone station to its new role as a tube station.** LT Museum

Facing page upper **An N7 tank engine moves gingerly over a temporary bridge across High Street, Wanstead (Snaresbrook station) during the replacement of the brick arch by a much longer steel girder bridge, 1946-47.** Desmond Croome collection

Facing page lower **The situation at Leytonstone from May to December 1947, with steam trains to Loughton, Epping and Ongar using platform 1, and the tube trains platforms 2 and 3.** C.R.L. Coles

A 2.31 mile extension allowed tube trains to reach Leytonstone via Leyton on 5th May 1947. From Leyton Junction, just west of Leyton station, tube trains ran over the first electrified section of the LNER Loughton and Ongar branch. The appearance of most stations was little altered from their steam train days, apart from the ubiquitous station name bull's-eyes, but Leytonstone was extensively rebuilt in connection with the new road underpass to eliminate the level crossing. There was a subsurface ticket hall and a pedestrian subway below the tracks. The up platform was converted to an island by fitting in an extra track behind it. Subsequently this layout was useful in regulating the westbound service by holding trains arriving from Epping or Hainault to depart in the correct sequence, but for the present the extra platform was used by LNER steam trains now running between Leytonstone and Loughton, Epping or Ongar, the first stage in such trains gradually being driven back to their last stronghold between Epping and Ongar. Tube services from Leytonstone were at two minute intervals in the peaks, five minutes off-peak.

The impressive station building at Hanger Lane, completed in 1949. LT Museum

Public attention was now diverted to west London, where the Great Western built the burrowing junction between the Ealing and Greenford branches west of North Acton, and replaced the tracks to Greenford which had been laid pre-war, removed for war purposes and reinstated. Public service on the 3.9 miles from North Acton station to Greenford began on 30th June 1947. All new stations on the western extension were in the open air, and were unfinished on opening day, with temporary staircases and station offices. All intermediate stations to West Ruislip had island platforms. Hanger Lane, in a cutting, had a complete set of temporary buildings replaced by a permanent circular subsurface ticket hall in 1949. Perivale (on embankment) had a permanent street-level ticket hall, but the absence of a planned row of shops to the south gave it an unfinished appearance. Greenford was unusual, being sited just west of the Great Western's triangular junction at the north end of the Castlebar loop, involving the construction of massive concrete viaducts and arches, brick arches and steel girder bridges. The island platform had a single track bay at the east end to accommodate the future GWR shuttle trains from Ealing Broadway via Castlebar Park which, together with the Central Line extension to West Ruislip, began to run on 21st November 1948. In the meantime they called at Greenford platforms on the main line, which could be reached by subway from the tube's street-level ticket hall. The island platform complex could be reached by a single escalator, the first on LT railways to take passengers *up* to trains. With the Central Line providing local services, the Great Western halts or platforms at Old Oak Lane, North Acton, Park Royal West, Brentham and Perivale were closed. Greenford had a 5-6 minute service in the peaks, $7^1/_2$-10 minute off-peak.

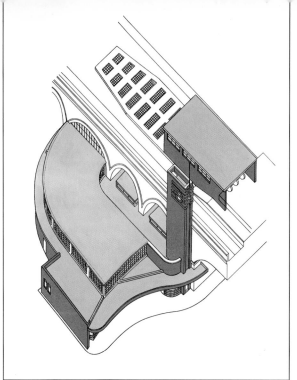

Stations on the western extension of the Central Line were designed by GWR architect Brian Lewis shortly before the war. When eventually rebuilt, a number of modifications were made. His design for Greenford was completed without the large tower.
David Lawrence

Below Two days before the opening of the extension from Greenford to West Ruislip, the Minister of Transport is about to open the way for a ceremonial train of standard stock.
LT Museum

White City platforms in May 1950. The station name bull's-eye has still not been finished, possibly because of the continuing severe steel shortage. LT Museum

The inadequacies of Wood Lane station and depot have been mentioned already. The platforms could not accommodate standard stock trains longer than six cars, and having three separate platforms (of which only one was straight) was not an efficient way to run a station. The solution was to build a new station 350 yards to the north, which had the advantage of being that much closer to White City stadium. Work began on 6th May 1946, and involved widening the cutting to accommodate a new two-platform (three-track) station, and improving the approach by building a new 220yd covered way for the westbound track, east of the old lines. The new station opened on 23rd November 1947, with a temporary ticket hall. A 447ft dead-end reversing siding, temporarily signalled from plungers at the ends of the platforms, was available just beyond the station, between the running lines. Subsequent developments in this area comprised the opening of White City signalbox and the middle track on 4th July 1948, of the new westbound covered way on 18th July, the closure of the Wood Lane station loop from 28th November 1948, and the completion of the final station layout and rebuilt sheds at White City depot (to give 14 regular stabling roads and two other sidings) in August and September 1949. The brick surface station won a Festival of Britain Award for Merit, the relevant plaque being visible on the street elevation. An auxiliary ticket office adjoined the main office, for crowds returning from events at White City stadium or Queens Park Rangers football ground. The first section of a subway beneath Wood Lane to the stadium was built, but was not completed owing to lack of external finance.

East Acton, with a standard stock train to West Ruislip departing. The spartan nature of the platform facilities shows that there has been little change since it opened in 1920.
John Gillham

Wood Lane depot, just before closure in that form in November 1948, showing the awkward layout. On the left, the old turntable is just visible to the right of the hut. LT Museum

Workmen converting the surface buildings at Wanstead for their peacetime role following their use during the war as a factory by the Plessey electronics company. LT Museum

Meanwhile intensive work had continued in the east, and the line openings of 14th December 1947 were publicised widely under the slogan 'Seven More Stations', with a 2.89 mile extension from Leytonstone to Woodford and 4.11 from Leytonstone to Newbury Park. Three of the new stations were on the Eastern Avenue tube, and each had distinctive features. Wanstead was of conventional pattern at tube level, but the box shaped ticket hall was adapted from wartime construction for the Plessey factory. Two escalators were installed but one was not available until 22nd February 1948. Redbridge was a cut and cover station, with the island platform being reached by stairs from the street, and at first had a temporary ticket hall. The permanent station was one of the last examples of Charles Holden's work for the London Underground. It opened in the following year, and had a circular ticket office, with shops and lavatories adjoining, and a square ventilation tower. Gants Hill station was famous for its long and lofty concourse between the tube level platforms, 150ft long and 20ft high, with a domed roof supported by two rows of eight tiled columns. Such a concourse was a useful device to clear passengers quickly from the platforms, valuable at stations where there were as many passengers boarding as alighting. At suburban Gants Hill it was a little extravagant, and the idea seems to have stemmed from a 1935 report by Underground engineers on the Moscow Metro, with an LT decision that it must have a Moscow type station somewhere. Three escalators rose 32ft 3in from the end of the concourse to the sub-surface ticket hall, which had subway connections to ten points round the large road intersection above. One escalator did not enter service until 14th March 1948.

For the extension from Leytonstone to Newbury Park, the opening ceremony was conducted at Wanstead, this being the first newly constructed station on this stretch of the line.
LT Museum

Boarding a westbound standard stock train at Wanstead in July 1949. The continuous station name frieze on tiles was a feature of a number of Underground stations completed between 1938 and 1947. Fluorescent lighting was being introduced on the Underground at the time of these extensions and the sub-surface stations on the Central Line east of Liverpool Street were the first tube stations to be equipped with it from new. LT Museum

The tube tracks south of Newbury Park station, descending and bearing right to run into tube tunnels towards Gants Hill. The ex-LNER goods line that formerly ran straight ahead to Seven Kings and Ilford was taken out of use in March 1956. *Alan A Jackson*

After Gants Hill, the tube tunnels curved first south east and then north, to break surface on each side of the LNER Fairlop loop tracks just south of Newbury Park, and connect into those tracks for through running. At Newbury Park the Great Eastern station buildings remained, but were supplemented by a new bus station east of the railway station and north of Eastern Avenue. This had a copper-covered barrel vault roof of reinforced concrete, and opened on 6th July 1949. It gained a Festival of Britain award for its designer. Housing development east of the station was restricted by town planning rules, so that the bus station did not realise its potential as a major tube/bus interchange, and was normally used by one or two routes in the eastbound direction only. For the railway station there was a new concrete footbridge and staircases to both platforms, a new station entrance and staff canteen (opened mid-1950), and a temporary ticket office. Otherwise the old platforms, buildings and canopies remained in use. At ground level a temporary fan of storage sidings for 10 trains was built. The Fairlop loop was electrified as far as Grange Hill for a limited number of empty trains to run between Hainault depot and Newbury Park. Both Woodford and Newbury Park had a four-minute peak service, $7\frac{1}{2}$ minutes off-peak.

When the dual carriageway road bridge for Eastern Avenue was built in 1957, the old GER ticket hall was demolished, but a permanent ticket office was not built until 1988. The steam passenger trains between Ilford and Woodford via Newbury Park ran for the last time on 29th November 1947, and were replaced by special buses from Ilford, calling at all stations to Roding Valley via Woodford. With the tube extension, the bus service was curtailed to run Newbury Park–Roding Valley via Woodford.

The Central Line extension from Leytonstone to Woodford served the intermediate stations of Snaresbrook and South Woodford, which were little changed from Great Eastern days, although they both had an additional ticket hall on the westbound side in 1948. Woodford station retained many of the Eastern Counties Railway and Great Eastern Railway buildings. It had been rebuilt between 1888 and 1892; for the arrival of the Central Line the westbound ticket hall was partly rebuilt and a brick building was added on the eastbound platform. The retreating LNER steam trains to Epping and Ongar terminated in platform 2 and the tube trains in platform 1, to give easy interchange.

Loughton station on first day of operation of tube trains, 21st November 1948. It had originally been intended that the London trains would terminate on the outside platforms and the shuttle to Ongar start from the middle track; this intention was implemented for 10 months with LNER steam trains. Each platform was sheltered by distinctive concrete canopies with rounded ends. LT Museum

These were the last Central Line extensions to be opened under the aegis of the LPTB and the main line railway companies, as all were swept into the nationalised British Transport Commission from 1st January 1948. Day-to-day control of the former LPTB operations was taken over by the London Transport Executive, and of the former railway companies by the Railway Executive, but the Commission (BTC) kept control of all major capital works.

The Newbury Park–Hainault section (1.91 miles) was opened for electric passenger service on 31st May 1948. The intermediate stations of Barkingside and Fairlop were little changed apart from retiling the ticket halls and extending the platforms. Hainault station was partly rebuilt, with a circular ticket hall and new waiting room. A new island platform replaced the old eastbound, and three girder bridges (five tracks) spanned New North Road to accommodate the platform tracks and a headshunt for Hainault depot. The depot had stabling space for 344 cars and had been completed in 1939; some of the standard stock cars stored there during the war had to be moved into the open when the US Army Transportation Corps took over the depot to assemble military rolling stock from June 1943 to January 1945. Reinstated for tube use, it comprised a nine-road car shed (with two roads straddled by a 15-ton travelling crane and all roads having pits long enough for a nine-car train), a three-road cleaning shed, washing plant and 16 open storage roads, 13 of which could hold two nine-car trains. Rail access was available from both the Grange Hill and Hainault station ends. Hainault had 17 trains per hour to London via Newbury Park in the peaks, and a $7^1/_2$-10 minute service off-peak.

The 21st November 1948 was a red letter day for the Central, for it witnessed the opening of more new tube mileage on one day than at any time since the Bakerloo extension to Watford Junction of April 1917. In the west tube trains were extended from Greenford to West Ruislip, and in the east from Woodford to Loughton and round the north side of the Fairlop loop from Woodford to Hainault. The western extension had been formally opened by the Minister of Transport two days before. One of the largest works had been the widening of the Northolt cutting, needing 37,000 cubic yards of clay to be removed over half a mile. The two new tracks continued from Greenford on the south side of the High Wycombe line, with intermediate stations at Northolt, South Ruislip and Ruislip Gardens. The proposal to continue to Denham was abandoned, as Green Belt legislation precluded any widespread housing development. The Western Region's steam railmotors from Ealing Broadway were cut back from West Ruislip to the central bay at Greenford. The island platforms on the extension had double curved reinforced concrete canopies 3¼in thick, on centre columns spaced at 24ft. Northolt and Ruislip Gardens had temporary ticket offices, whilst at South Ruislip and West Ruislip the new ticket offices were left half finished. Permanent ticket halls were not provided until 1961-62. West Acton, on the Ealing branch, had fared better, as its neat box-shaped brick and glass ticket hall had opened in November 1940. West Ruislip had a 10-12 minute service of tube trains.

Between Ruislip Gardens and West Ruislip was Ruislip depot, which had been almost completed by the GWR by 1939 and had been requisitioned by the Admiralty for contractors (Birmingham Small Arms) to make anti-aircraft guns. It had space for 472 cars (184 under cover and the rest in open sidings) and was designed to share with Hainault the tasks of cleaning and maintaining the Central Line fleet. As with Hainault, rail access could be obtained from either end. On 20th November 1948, 200 tons of machinery were transferred from White City (Wood Lane) depot to Ruislip, and part of the old depot was rebuilt as a stabling and storage facility. At the western end of West Ruislip station there was a physical connection to the High Wycombe line to receive new rolling stock, to send old stock away for scrap, and to despatch stock for rehabilitation and receive it back.

The former Fairlop loop became the Hainault loop under LT, with the tracks designated as 'inner' or 'outer rail', as on the Circle Line. The top of the loop was opened to tube trains concurrently with the Loughton extension, with 3.8 miles of newly served track. The first station, Roding Valley, had been opened by the LNER as a halt on 3rd February 1936, but was rebuilt in a pleasant lightweight style for tube trains, completed in 1949. Chigwell was heavily reconstructed, but retained much of its original Great Eastern style. Grange Hill was heavily and unsympathetically reconstructed in 1948. It served the new Hainault LCC estate and, as at Chigwell, the platforms were extended for eight-car tube trains. The shuttle service between Hainault and Woodford ran at 7½ minute intervals, peak, 10 minutes off-peak.

Considerable high level discussion was devoted to the merits of the further extension from Loughton to Epping, but the presence of some housing estates, including the large new LCC estate at Debden with over 4000 housing units, and the partly completed electrification, swung the decision in favour of continuing. The 4.9 route miles from Loughton were served by tube trains from 25th September 1949, with intermediate stations at Chigwell Lane (renamed Debden concurrently with the extension) and Theydon Bois. At these stations and the Epping terminus, the GER buildings were little altered except for ticket hall reconstruction, and installation of electric light and LT signs. At Debden, two sidings were added between the running lines. At Epping, tube trains normally terminated in the eastbound platform and steam shuttles to Ongar in the westbound, involving a climb across the footbridge for through passengers.

Through trains from Epping to London at first were at 40 or 48 minute intervals in the off-peak, supplemented by a shuttle service of short trains to Loughton at the same frequencies. There was a 10-15 minute service of through trains in the peaks. From Debden to Loughton there was a 10-12 minute service in the off-peak and a six minute one in the peaks.

The last day of steam operation on the Epping-Ongar line, 16th November 1957, showing a train at North Weald. Alan A. Jackson

The same location a few years later with a 1935 tube stock two-car train at work. A level crossing just north of this station remained in use until the line's closure in 1994. Frank Mussett

From 25th September 1949, the Epping–Ongar section was transferred to London Transport administration, with steam shuttles being worked by BR on behalf of LT. Finally, the Government accepted the LT argument that if this section was to continue to have a railway service, 'light electrification' was the cheapest long-term option. Two-car tube shuttles first ran on 18th November 1957, finally displacing steam from all-day passenger services. Intermediate stations were at Blake Hall and North Weald. This section will be reviewed in detail later.

Ownership of the Central Line extensions from Leyton Junction to Ongar, from Woodford to Newbury Park and from North Acton to West Ruislip was formally transferred from BR to London Transport on 23rd January 1950. On the eastern extensions, transfer of management was undertaken in stages, completed with the Loughton–Ongar section on 25th September 1949. It was also staged in the west, the final change being the transfer of staffing of stations from Greenford to West Ruislip to London Transport from 13th November 1967.

New signalboxes were provided at White City, North Acton (with the junction remotely controlled from White City), Greenford and West Ruislip, with a subsidiary frame at Ruislip Gardens (controlled from West Ruislip). In the east, new signalboxes or frames were provided at Bethnal Green, Leyton, Leytonstone, Newbury Park, Hainault, South Woodford, Woodford, Loughton, Debden and Epping, with a subsidiary frame at Grange Hill.

Rolling Stock Problems

As mentioned earlier, the arrival of 1938 stock on the Northern and Bakerloo Lines gave rise to a flow of standard stock that was earmarked for the extended Central Line. All the reallocated cars were overhauled and modernised at Acton Works, enabling the Liverpool Street–Ealing Broadway line to be operated entirely with six-car trains of standard stock from 11th June 1939. The modernisation included adding retardation control to the electro-pneumatic brakes, and weak field flag switches for higher speeds on the open sections. Passenger door control was also fitted, but not used at that time.

The cars not immediately required on the Central Line had to be stored elsewhere on the system. The nearly completed Hainault and Ruislip depots took many, but wartime requisitioning of depot space forced many other cars into open air storage; this also applied generally to the other storage sites at Edgware, Golders Green, Highgate, Morden, Neasden and Stanmore. When the time approached to use the 340 stored cars for their intended purpose, they first had to undergo extensive renovation at Acton Works to remedy the effects of prolonged open-air storage and vandalism, including complete electrical rewiring. Despite these heroic efforts, they became unreliable in service. The timetable of 14th December 1947 specified that 67 trains should run in the Monday to Friday peaks, including 12 eight-car trains. Unreliability compelled a reduction to two such trains in the following month, and the target of 12 was not achieved until May 1948. Maintaining trains in the cramped Wood Lane depot was very difficult, but the position improved slightly when Hainault depot came fully into use in May 1948 and Ruislip in November.

Two pre-war operational practices were re-introduced for relatively short periods. Running shorter trains in the off-peak periods (known internally as 'uncoupling') was introduced on the Central Line on 19th February 1951, and passenger door control on 25th October 1948.

The abandonment of a pre-war scheme to run nine-car trains on the Northern Line had left a fleet of 1938 stock without the correct proportions of types of car (driving motor, trailer etc) to run standard seven-car trains. Therefore an order was placed in June 1950 for 91 new cars to correct the imbalance, which were later known as 1949 stock. The effect was to allow fifteen 1938 stock trains to be introduced on the Piccadilly Line between 1951 and 1953, thus releasing the Piccadilly's more modern standard stock for use on the Central. The oldest cars were scrapped or used for engineers' trains, and the Central was able to run 33 eight-car trains by November 1952 and 48 by November 1957.

The six flat-ended cars of the experimental 1935 order were re-equipped to be similar to 1938 stock, and allocated to run as two-car units on the Loughton–Epping and Hainault–Woodford shuttles. They had all arrived on the Central by February 1951, but were removed in May 1954 for use on the Holborn–Aldwych shuttle, and their duties taken over by standard stock sets. Two units were moved back to the Central for the electrification to Ongar of November 1957.

A number of former standard stock control trailers had been converted into plain trailers shortly after the war, leaving the cabs as wasted space. Between 1955 and 1958, the cab space was merged into the main saloon, providing four extra seats on the 71 cars that were converted.
LT Museum

A 1952 plan for new trains to replace the rest of the Piccadilly Line's standard stock (and so release modern standard stock for the Central) was defeated by labour and material shortages, but replacement of all the standard stock could not be deferred indefinitely and so a further plan was devised, to have modernised trains specially designed for the Central Line. Each of the 84$^1/_2$ trains would have comprised eight cars, consisting of four new driving motor cars of what became known as 1960 stock and four extensively renovated trailer cars from the Piccadilly Line's standard stock fleet. As the trailer cars in the new trains would have had four doors each side to avoid boarding delays, any existing two-door trailers taken over would have required the addition of two doors each side. The new cars were built by Cravens of Sheffield, and incorporated several new features such as two-motor bogies and panoramic side windows, fluorescent lighting and door fault indicator lights. They had unpainted aluminium alloy bodies and roof panels. Three such trains were built as an experiment, and the first entered service on 9th November 1960. They originally ran on the main Central Line services, but were later relegated to the shuttles.

Meanwhile a new plan to renew the Piccadilly Line fleet had been proceeding separately. Three experimental seven-car trains by different makers (known as '1956 stock') had entered service by April 1958. They incorporated some major advances such as rubber suspension, unpainted aluminium alloy bodies, and internal fluorescent lighting. They were soon followed by an order for 76 similar trains (532 cars) to oust all the remaining standard stock on the Piccadilly Line. The Central Line would have benefited from the transfer of more modern standard stock from the Piccadilly, both by the increased reliability of newer stock and by strengthening all its 'main line' trains to eight cars. This process began soon after the first 1959 stock began work on the Piccadilly. In due course the Central would have had its own 1960 stock.

Standard stock trains being maintained in Ruislip depot in April 1955. LT Museum

This plan was overtaken by events. On 28th July 1958 there was a fire in a cable 'receptacle box' of a standard stock train near Holland Park station, in which 51 passengers and staff had to be treated in hospital and one passenger later died from fumes. On 11th August 1960 there was a similar fire near Redbridge, which caused 41 people to be admitted to hospital. The 1958 fire had shown that if the guard isolated the passenger door control circuits in emergency, he also cut out the emergency light and telephone communication with the driver and the controller. The passenger door control system (which had also proved troublesome in other ways) was therefore rendered inoperative on all lines from the end of March 1959. 'Uncoupling' to provide shorter trains in off-peaks was also felt to have net disadvantages, and was withdrawn on the Central Line from January 1960. It was then possible to give attention to the long space without doors in the middle of an eight-car train, caused by two motor cars being coupled nose to nose. In effect, one four-car unit was split in two, and half coupled at each end of another four-car unit, giving the formation M-T+ M-T-T-M+T-M.

A 1960 stock train in the days when it was used for Central main line service, with two standard stock trailers between the two motor cars of each unit. Desmond Croome

The two fires and increasing breakdowns and delays had added urgency to the need to replace the standard stock, coupled with the prospect of BR's electrification in 1960 of the Hackney Downs group of lines adding more Central Line traffic west of Liverpool Street. Furthermore, reconditioning the trailer cars for the 1960 trains had proved very expensive. Therefore the flow of 1959 stock was diverted to the Central after 19 trains had been delivered to the Piccadilly, and 57 extra non-driving motor cars were ordered to make trains up to eight cars. The first (seven-car) 1959 stock train entered service on the Central on 19th April 1960. By asking the manufacturers to concentrate on making four-car units of 1959 stock, the first eight-car 1959 stock train ran on the Central on 25th July 1960, which also saw the remainder of the Central's standard stock trains augmented to eight-car. The first of the 57 extra cars ran on the Central Line on 25th May 1961, and the order for these cars, and the balance of the 1959 stock, was completed in February 1962.

The interior of a 1960 stock motor car, ideas from which were used on the 1967 design for the Victoria Line. LT Museum

If there was any conflict within London Transport's rolling stock department between the traditionalists and the innovators, it was settled in favour of the former by an autumn 1960 order for another 619 cars of what later became known as 1962 stock. This was almost identical to 1959 stock, but had some minor technical improvements. The order was later augmented by three trains (24 cars) to release the 1960 trains for the shuttles and three cars for the Aldwych branch of the Piccadilly. The 57 extra cars ordered earlier were also grouped with the 1962 stock, so the total 1962 fleet comprised 703 cars. The first complete 1962 stock train ran on the Central on 12th April 1962, and all 1962 stock was in service by 29th June 1964. With the build-up of 1962 stock, some standard stock was transferred back to the Piccadilly, and subsequently the 1959 trains were also moved there to join the original 19. The final standard stock train was withdrawn from the main Central Line by the end of December 1962, and from the shuttles on 14th June 1963. At last the Central Line main line operations had a standardised fleet of modern rolling stock.

Looking west towards North Acton station, with the North London Line bridge above, the Victoria Road bridge in the middle distance, and the main High Wycombe line at a higher level on the right. The first 1959 stock train had entered service on the Central Line on 19th April 1960, and the two freight tracks on the right were taken out of use in March 1964. In the meantime, a pannier tank heads towards the West London Line, whilst a train of empty milk tanks hauled by diesel loco D862 heads west. J J Smith

Interior of 1959 stock on the Central Line, virtually identical to the 1962 stock which became the mainstay of the Central fleet for 30 years.
LT Museum

Freight operation on the eastern end of the Central suffered progressive reductions, starting with the relatively minor inconvenience of cutting the Newbury Park–Seven Kings connection on 19th March 1956. After this, freight yards on the Ongar line and the Hainault loop closed gradually, from Fairlop in March 1958 to the final batch on 18th April 1966, comprising yards at Woodford, Loughton, Debden, Theydon Bois, Epping, Blake Hall and Ongar. The connection to BR at Leyton Junction was used by early morning steam trains until 2nd November 1959 and diesel powered passenger trains until 31st May 1970 (from Epping or Loughton to Stratford or Liverpool Street), when buses were substituted pending official approval for BR to abandon these services. The signal cabin at Leyton was closed from 5th November 1971 and the connection physically broken on 29th October 1972, completing a further step in isolating the London Transport system from BR. When operating on the Central Line, a speed limit of 20mph had applied to BR trains.

With the post-war economic recovery, a start could be made on some planned or part-finished station schemes. A new ticket hall beneath Liverpool Street had come into service on 19th February 1951 and a new subway below Broad Street station forecourt to the old CLR ticket hall allowed the 1912 escalators to be withdrawn. Bank ticket hall was retiled and redecorated in 1961-62, and, at low level, had improved interchange between the Central and Northern Lines in 1972 when part of a second lift shaft was equipped with spiral stairs, thus providing one-way flow in each staircase. Road widening at St Paul's resulted in construction of a new entrance to the subsurface ticket hall, completed in 1973. The City of London footed the bill. Tottenham Court Road ticket hall was modernised in 1974.

Standard type of train indicator installed on the central part of the line – large, but with very small lettering. The central section was intended for general information
LT Museum

Despite the installation of high speed automatic lifts in 1942, Oxford Circus had long been severely congested in the evening rush hour. Construction of the Victoria Line in the mid-1960s gave the opportunity to build a new ticket hall beneath the Circus, with stairways to street level at each quadrant. At most times the new ticket hall was used for incoming passengers and the old ticket hall for those leaving the station. From the new concourse a wide subway led towards the Bakerloo and Victoria Lines, but Central Line passengers turned right to use a single escalator that had been built through Peter Robinson's second basement. The new ticket hall and three of the quadrant stairwells opened on 30th September 1968, with seven out of the nine new escalators. The rest were ready for the formal opening of the Victoria Line on 7th March 1969. The lifts were taken out of use in December 1968.

Bond Street, one station west of Oxford Circus, also benefited from the opening of a new line. The scheme for an interchange station with the Jubilee Line involved trebling the size of the ticket hall, installing three new escalators to connect the Jubilee Line to the Central Line concourse, and three more to the ticket hall. A new subway running north beneath Oxford Street gave traffic-free access to Stratford Place. Most of the works were ready for the Jubilee opening on 1st May 1979, but the permanent ticket office opened in June 1980.

Queensway (renamed from Queen's Road in 1946) acquired Wadsworth high speed automatic lifts in 1956-57. Reconditioning of the Holland Park Sprague lifts was completed in July 1959, and of those at Lancaster Gate in 1960-61, where a traffic management scheme completed in 1968 involved demolishing the old surface buildings and incorporating the ticket hall in the Royal Lancaster Hotel.

At Notting Hill Gate, a combined Central and Circle Line station with escalators had been authorised in the LPTB Act of 1937. Some work began in summer 1938 but was stopped by the war. Post-war restrictions on capital expenditure caused further postponement, but an LCC road widening scheme was the catalyst that allowed progress. The scheme provided a ticket hall beneath the roadway, with subway and staircase connections to surrounding pavements. Escalator panelling was in satin finished aluminium, and ceilings were lined with pastel grey, pink and yellow plastic sheeting. Interchange subways and landings were finished with high gloss tiles, either rich wine red with black relief, or sky blue. Fluorescent lighting was used throughout. Most of the new station opened on 1st March 1959, but the lowest escalators were not ready until 31st July 1960.

Reconstruction and redevelopment at Ealing Broadway provided a new ticket hall for all lines, with the BR and Central Line sections opening on 5th December 1965 and staffed by BR ticket clerks. In the east, Debden station was rebuilt in 1973-74 with an enlarged ticket hall and new platform canopies, lighting and staff accommodation.

The Central Line did not require major signalling improvements in the 1950s or 1960s, but in 1952 Ealing Broadway benefited from a push-button route-setting frame with remote control interlocking, controlling the Central and District terminal operations. This cabin was closed in 1974 with the centralisation of District Line signalling, but the Central Line section of the interlocking machine room was now controlled by push button from White City. Normally the terminal reversing at Ealing Broadway was automatic. White City push buttons also controlled North Acton junction and crossover, modernised in 1973. Miniature lever power frames replaced 'mechanical' frames at Bank in 1958, Marble Arch in 1956 and Queensway in 1957, but the Bank box and crossover were closed in October 1970, and the Queensway box and siding in July 1982.

A 1967 stock train on trial on the Hainault-Woodford shuttle, about to leave Hainault.
Desmond Croome

The distribution of traffic on the Central Line continued to follow the same pattern as when the extensions first opened – moderately heavy south of Woodford and Hainault, very heavy on the Leyton–Liverpool Street section, and continuing through the centre to Shepherd's Bush, fairly heavy out to Ealing Broadway and to Northolt, but generally lighter on the western suburban section than on the eastern, and with the Mile End–Liverpool Street–Bank section being critical.

Construction of the Victoria Line had been sanctioned by the Government in 1962, and LT hoped to use a form of Automatic Train Operation, in which the trains would effectively drive themselves. After some limited experiments on the District Line, the Woodford–Hainault section of the Central was chosen as the test bed. The three 8-car trains of 1960 stock were split into six 4-car units, and five of these were converted to receive commands from the trackside to accelerate or brake according to the coded impulses transmitted through the running rails. Other alterations were made to permit one-person operation. The first converted train entered service on 5th April 1964, and by March 1965 the system had been proved reliable enough to be specified for the new stock for the Victoria Line ('1967 stock'). From 1967 this stock began to arrive at Ruislip depot to have motors and equipment fitted, and most of the new trains were transferred to Hainault depot for about three weeks for testing between Woodford and Hainault. A few stayed much longer, but traffic demands on the Victoria Line caused the last 1967 train to leave Hainault in September 1984. Duties on the shuttle then reverted to 1960 stock, but breakdowns were covered by 4-car 1962 stock trains with guards. The 1960 stock was whittled down by scrappings or diversion to the engineers' fleet, so that by 1983 only three 3-car trains were left, with the two standard stock trailers in each unit having been replaced by one 1938 stock trailer. The Woodford–Hainault branch was also used briefly for trials, but not in passenger service, of Fully Automatic Control of Trains, requiring no-one in the cab. These trials took place in 1978. From 20th October 1986, train radio was fitted to permit conventional OPO, and the ATO on the branch decommissioned.

During these years there were changes of control from the centre. The London Transport Executive survived until the last day of 1962, but on the following day was replaced by the London Transport Board, reporting direct to the Minister of Transport. This régime lasted seven years, to be replaced from 1st January 1970 by a new London Transport Executive, reporting to the Greater London Council, but with central government retaining control of major capital expenditure. An interesting period lay ahead.

Modernised Stations

A comprehensive plan to renew the rolling stock and signalling, power supply and control of the Central Line was put to the Greater London Council in October 1982, but it was several years before there was any visible evidence of activity. There was, in fact, a planned seven-year gap between major rolling stock orders, and in 1981 the GLC approved a 10-year programme to modernise 140 stations. About two thirds of the expenditure was to be made on 16 major schemes at busy points, where the best prospects existed to attract extra passengers. The Central Line's prime central position was recognised by selecting several of its stations for early treatment.

There was extensive platform and concourse redecoration at central London stations, most notably Tottenham Court Road, Oxford Circus, Bond Street and Marble Arch; new Wadsworth lifts were installed at Lancaster Gate, Queensway and Holland Park from 1988, 1983/4 and 1987 respectively.

Decorative tiling at the modernised Bond Street platform on the Central Line has a 'wrapping paper' theme. Capital Transport

Mosaic tiles at Tottenham Court Road, another of the station modernisations of the 1980s.
Capital Transport

Improvements at Liverpool Street complemented the complete reconstruction of the main line station. The escalators between the Central and Circle Lines were renewed and the fixed stairway replaced by a third escalator. A large new combined Central/Circle ticket hall was a few steps down from the main line concourse. The original Central London Railway ticket hall was greatly enlarged and the escalators renewed; three additional escalators linked this ticket hall to a cross passage at the eastern end of the Central Line platforms, which helped distribute passengers more evenly along them. This work started in February 1986 and was finished in May 1992.

In the eastern suburbs, Mile End platforms, stairs and ticket hall were retiled, mostly in green and cream. False ceilings, new lighting and enamelled white panels behind the Central Line tracks completed the redecoration, which took from 1987 to 1991.

Train indicators comprising a matrix of yellow light-emitting diodes came to the Underground in 1983-86, after limited experiments in 1980-81. These showed the destinations of the first, second and third trains, and how many minutes away they were, and could also be used to show standard or special messages. On the Central, their installation was initially confined to the Marble Arch–Stratford section.

Free-standing ticket offices known as 'passimeters' had been introduced in the 1920s, in the days when ticket checking was meticulous. They had the advantage that booking clerks could also, at slack times, collect the tickets of passengers who had completed their journeys. By the 1930s these extra duties had been abandoned at most stations, but passimeters were still favoured as being on a passenger's direct line of route. However, by the early 1980s, security considerations and the desire to improve working conditions gave rise to a programme to replace passimeters by wall ticket offices from 1982, although this had a rather slow start. The changes known collectively as the Underground Ticketing System had an even slower start, but the reconstruction of all ticket offices to the 'wall' type (incorporating ticket-issuing machines) and installation of ticket-checking gates at all Fare Zone 1 stations began in earnest in early 1986.

Ruislip depot has always had excess capacity, and since 1956 has been used for the reception and commissioning of most new surface and tube rolling stock. The western half of the lifting shop, under the 15-ton crane runways, was reserved for this task. Part of the site was also used for permanent way work, beginning with a rail welding plant, and developed into a £4.2 million depot to assemble pre-formed track lengths. To give the permanent way trains a shorter route to many of their working sites, a rail link was constructed from the western end of Ruislip depot to the Metropolitan Line's Uxbridge branch west of Ruislip, together with a reversing siding. This opened in July 1973, was signalled in summer 1975, and the siding was used by short-working Piccadilly Line trains from 21st February 1977. Subsequently Ruislip's association with engineering work was further developed with the concentration there of modernisation and maintenance of engineers' rolling stock, performed in the western half of the lifting shop.

The turmoil arising from the GLC-imposed fare reductions of October 1981, increases from March 1982 and reductions from May 1983 had strengthened the Government's view that the GLC was not the best body to control London Transport. Direct Government control was re-established with the formation of London Regional Transport from 29th June 1984. A subsidiary body, London Underground Ltd, started trading on 1st April 1985.

Control of London Transport by the GLC had indirectly affected the fate of the Epping–Ongar section, which was well outside the GLC area, but we must first recall the early days of electric operation.

At first, the third 1935 stock train was kept back for test train duties, and its place taken on the Ongar line by a three-car train of 1938 stock. From June 1958, the 1935 stock motor cars had had a 1927 vintage trailer car inserted between them. In 1960 a third 1935 stock train, with trailer, was available for the branch, and the 1938 stock train returned to the Northern Line. The 1935/1927 trains were painted silver to match the new 1962 stock, the first entering service in August 1963. However they were becoming progressively more unreliable, and from December 1966 were replaced by four-car trains of 1962 stock, specially modified to limit the current demanded.

From 18th April 1966 the Ongar goods yard closed, and in 1970 came London Transport's first proposal to close the whole line east of Epping. This was refused by the Government in April 1972, but without any grant to cover the revenue losses. In the mid-1970s London Transport was involved in prolonged negotiations with the County Councils beyond the GLC boundary for them to offer some financial support, but little support was forthcoming. Reduction in Government revenue support for London Transport caused it to reduce the service to a one-train operation from 18th October 1976. The North Weald loop was lifted in the following year. London Transport also tried to reduce the deficit by raising the out-county fares beyond standard. In 1980 the single fare from Ongar to Woodford was £2.20, only 40p less than that to West Ruislip or Amersham. A further closure proposal was lodged in May 1980 but this was refused in March 1981, although closure of Blake Hall station was approved. This station was last open on 31st October 1981. The train service to North Weald and Ongar was reduced to Monday to Friday peaks only on 6th December 1982, but a last attempt was made to boost traffic by re-introducing a daily, all day service from 30th October 1989.

However, this worthy effort failed to stem the decline in patronage, and the service reverted to Monday to Friday peaks only from 8th April 1991.

Blake Hall station on the Ongar branch in the final week of the station's operation. A four-car train of 1962 stock provides more than adequate accommodation. David Stuttard

During the 1980s some interesting proposals were made which could have affected the Central Line profoundly if implemented. A 1986 study looked at numerous ways to exploit light rail in the London area. It listed for further examination the conversion to light rail of the Central Line sections between West Ruislip and Greenford, Woodford and Hainault, and Woodford and Ongar. Nothing more was heard of this idea, which seems likely to have achieved economies, but at the expense of passengers having to change trains at the interface between modes, and depots having to maintain two types of rolling stock.

The Central London Rail Study of 1989 suggested a new Central Line branch from Shepherd's Bush via the Goldhawk and Bath Roads to Turnham Green, continuing to Richmond to take over the District service (a near-identical resurrection of the 1913 proposal). The Bakerloo would have had a new branch from Queen's Park to North Acton, to take over the Central's Ealing Broadway service.

An alteration of lesser magnitude was the abolition of the separate Hainault–Woodford shuttle, partly achieved on 8th April 1991 and completely on 2nd November 1992, when some of the trains terminating at Hainault from the south were projected to Woodford to cover this section.

Full Modernisation

Pending the receipt of Government approval for the Central Line modernisation scheme, it was desirable that new ideas in rolling stock design should be tried in full scale tests. In March 1983 three four-car trains were ordered, of different designs and with different manufacturers participating. They were delivered between October 1986 and March 1987, and were shown to Central Line passengers in a static display at Woodford in June 1987. Staff and passengers were asked to indicate their preferences for the numerous innovative design features. The new trains (known as '1986 stock') were formally launched into passenger service on the Jubilee Line in May 1988, running in six-car formation, but the experiment came to a slightly premature end with a derailment of one of them just north of Neasden station on 14th August 1989.

Government approval for the £720 million scheme to renew the rolling stock and signalling of the Central Line was given in October 1988, and the contract for new signalling was placed in October 1989. The cost rose to £750m by 1991.

In the meantime, after a review of safety precautions following the King's Cross fire of 1987, the 1962 stock was modified in 1989-90 to replace the passenger alarm handles (which directly applied the brakes) by passenger alarm buttons which merely alerted the driver to a problem. Other alterations included fitting public address from the driver, removing hazardous interior materials, and fitting more powerful headlights.

Interior of the 'Green Train' of 1986 stock, on display at Woodford in June 1987 (Metro-Cammell body with Brown Boveri equipment). Desmond Croome

In many respects, the new signalling authorised in 1988 was a modernised and computerised version of the Victoria Line's, but had features added to check how the service was running and to initiate remedial action. The train operator would open and close the doors at stations, and could drive the train manually if necessary, without being restricted to the speed limits that applied automatically on the Victoria Line.

With the combined benefits of new signalling and new trains, it was hoped to be able to run up to 34 or 35 trains per hour, with line capacity increased by 16% and a 12% reduction in journey times. The resignalling started at the West Ruislip end, and went hand in hand with track rationalisation and improvements including an extra track at North Acton to give additional reversing facilities from the east. Other features of the scheme included an enhanced power supply (with new and enlarged substations), some realignment of tunnel segments and tunnel tracks to improve the clearances for the new trains, and a new high security control and signalling centre at Wood Lane.

The order for 85 eight-car trains was placed with BREL (later taken over by ABB) in September 1989, with 20 further cars ordered for the Waterloo & City Line. The traction equipment was to be supplied by a consortium of ABB and Brush Electrical Machines. The London Underground trains were later known as '1992 stock' and their design made use of the experience gained with the 1986 trains. An eight-car train weighed 173 tons, 32 tons less than the 1962 stock it replaced.

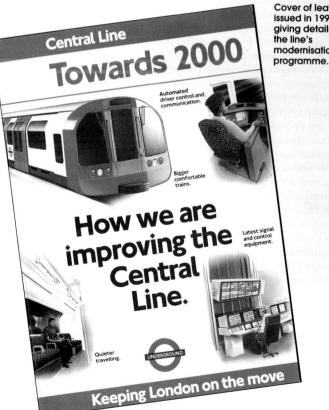

Cover of leaflet issued in 1990 giving details of the line's modernisation programme.

The car bodies were fabricated from welded aluminium extrusions to form body shells, with eight extrusions for the floor and four for the roof. Because of dense passenger traffic on the central London section, the design provided for the double doors to give a greater opening (5ft 5¹/₂ins wide). This needed special reinforcement in the bottom corners of the door openings. As it would have been difficult to provide door pockets in bodies assembled from extrusions, the doors are hung externally; internal stiffening with aluminium honeycomb gives a light, rigid structure. The doors are suspended from stainless steel rods, and guided at solebar level by polyurethane rollers. The door engines are mounted under adjacent seats, and transmit movement to the doors by a rod through the body side and the usual arm working in an arc of a circle. Passenger door control buttons are fitted, with 'open' buttons in the middle of the door separations, inside and out, and 'open' and 'close' buttons inside in the stand-back pillars. For single leaf doors, the 'open' buttons are body mounted.

The bogies are of the welded H frame, box section type, for strength and lightness. Kawasaki were chosen for producing the best designed bogie then available. Primary suspension is of the conventional rubber chevron type, and secondary by pneumatic air bags to keep the car floor at nearly constant height irrespective of passenger load. An over-inflation monitoring device is included to prevent the car body rising above loading gauge.

Each train has 32 d.c. traction motors supplied by ABB Switzerland. The design allows tractive effort to be more closely related to demands, and power consumption is about 40% lower than with 1962 stock. The small size of the motors allows them to be mounted on the bogie frame, so that they receive no shock loads (as happened with an axle hung motor) and the unsprung weight is reduced. The drive is through gearboxes and a flexible coupling.

The Westinghouse analogue braking system incorporates air brakes, and regenerative and rheostatic electric. Regenerative braking is the normal mode, but if train equipment finds that the supply system is not receptive to current, the train's on-board computer changes to the rheostatic mode. The final stop is made by a blend of electric and air braking.

Each train has only two cabs, to reduce costs and maximise passenger capacity. The train operator controls his train (in the manual mode) by a 'fore and aft' traction/brake controller with a rotating deadman's safety device. Closed circuit television is fitted in the cabs so that the operator can observe the side of a train at a station

Information is transmitted to each train by induction loops in the track, not only for safety of train movements and automatic operation but also to control door opening at stations, to activate the pre-recorded announcements and to convey messages from the Line Controller. There is also feed-back from the train to the Controller, including train identification details and passenger loads.

With the 1992 stock having so many innovative features, there was a long period of pre-service testing after the first four-car unit arrived at Ruislip on 17th May 1992. The first train entered public service on 7th April 1993, running in off-peak periods between West Ruislip and Liverpool Street. By 30th April 1994, fifty-nine new trains had been commissioned and about 46 were normally in service; by 16th October 60 trains of 1992 stock were scheduled and 11 of 1962, although teething troubles meant that real performance of the new trains tended to lag behind these aspirations. One-person operation was introduced in three stages, on 14th March, 24th July and 16th October 1994, and the very last Central Line 1962 stock train ran on the evening of 17th February 1995.

The final train of 1962 stock on the Central Line, seen at Loughton on 17th February 1995 before its last trip to West Ruislip. R J Greenaway

The arrival of new stock at Ruislip depot was complemented by an inevitable movement in the other direction, of 1962 stock to the scrap yard, but 7½ trains escaped this fate for a few years by being transferred for further service on the Northern Line and some others were retained for engineering duties.

The whole Central Line renewal was publicised under the slogan 'Towards 2000', with posters explaining that although everything would be fine in the long run, the work would entail temporary weekend closures for engineering work. These duly took place, but numerous mishaps during late 1993 and 1994 tried the patience of regular passengers. There were several derailments, mostly involving the 1992 stock, and often involving suspending the service for half a day. A derailment near Holborn on 16th October 1994 caused the evacuation of over 350 passengers.

A more widespread problem was excessive rail wear, attributed to the interaction between the sides of the rails and the flanges of the 1992 stock. The normal flange lubrication was overwhelmed by a sudden influx of new trains, and it had not been possible to apply enough additional grease in time. All this stock was withdrawn during the morning of 19th November 1993, with an emergency timetable using 1962 stock between West Ruislip and Epping, and Ealing and Hainault or Woodford via Grange Hill. Several lengthy speed restrictions were enforced and the service was suspended between Marble Arch and Leytonstone on Sunday 21st November 1993 to allow 1,700 metres of rail at seven sites to be replaced, and for the 1992 stock to resume work the next day. However worse trouble was to follow starting on the 23rd. A transient current supply failure occurred in the evening but a temporary supply was switched in and there was only a short delay. On the next day (Wednesday 24th November) the main supply failed in the morning peak and the back up supply failed too. A major power failure immobilised much of the Central Line and also the sub-

A train of 1992 stock at White City, one of a fleet of 85 eight-car trains. Built by ABB Transportation, they were delivered between May 1992 and March 1995. Each train has 32 motored axles, controlled by thyristors. The car bodies are formed of aluminium extrusions, and the sliding doors are hung externally. The double doors open to give a clear width of 5ft 5½in. Capital Transport

surface lines. 20,000 passengers were evacuated from trains stalled between stations, and as many as 300,000 were affected in all. An earth fault occurred at Newbury Park, which damaged cabling at Lots Road, and caused the Mile End switch house to shut down. Supplies to other lines were isolated and restored, and attention concentrated on restoring the Central Line supply. This was achieved in the evening peak of 24th November but failed again. Central Line services east of Liverpool Street were cancelled from the morning of 25th November 1993 and buses substituted for five days, using altogether 80 vehicles. Seventeen gangs were employed in tracing the primary fault, which was found 25ft above ground at Lots Road power station.

There were also numerous signal failures in December 1993 and January 1994, and yet another problem occurred in mid-morning on 14th February, when a dislodged current rail at St Paul's westbound caused several trains to lose their collector shoes; the service was suspended for the rest of the day between Liverpool Street and Marble Arch. The problem was repeated almost identically on Sunday 20th February, with service suspension on the central section for the rest of the day. Because some trains could not collect power, they had to be pushed back to Ruislip depot, with some occasional 24-car combinations evident. The 1992 stock collector shoes were urgently redesigned.

Problems with the resignalling were to continue, somewhat tarnishing the image of the line's modernisation and delaying the full commissioning of the new central control room.

Interior view of the 1992 tube stock. The seating has been criticised as less comfortable than other Underground stock; slim armrests were fitted at first but these were subjected to vandalism. Capital Transport

In its latter years the Epping-Ongar service was often worked by a train of 1960 stock, which had been painted red in 1990. In this view, the train approaches the Epping end of the branch. The middle car is a converted 1938 stock trailer. Desmond Croome

A side effect of the preparations for privatisation of British Rail was that the Waterloo & City Line, tenaciously retained by the Southern Railway and BR in all previous reorganisations, was transferred to London Transport from 1st April 1994. LT placed it under Central Line management, which was appropriate, as the Waterloo & City had just acquired a new fleet of 20 cars identical to the Central's new stock apart from the livery. The line closed down over the Easter weekend, so that BR's last day of operation was 31st March 1994 and LT's first 5th April. The train operations staff now came under control of Leytonstone, and the depot staff of Hainault. The line had its own LUL working timetable which recorded the end-to-end distance as 1.38 miles. Superficial alterations to the cars to demonstrate their new owners included removing the BR Network SouthEast flash, and adding Underground roundels to the car sides. Full Central Line diagrams were displayed inside. From July 1994, a Leytonstone driver's roster covered an average of one week's work on the W&C and two on the Central. The station fittings and signs were gradually brought into line with the Underground's.

On the antiquated north-eastern outpost of the Central Line, the Epping-Ongar branch, London Underground had made its third closure proposal in May 1993, stating that daily passenger trips had dropped to 100 from 750 in 1971. Each passenger was subsidised by £7.00 per return trip. As usual, implementation of the legal provisions for considering closures, and subsequent Ministerial rumination, took some time, but the Secretary of State for Transport gave permission for closure on 1st September 1994, and the final train to be operated on the line by London Underground left Ongar for Epping at 7.15pm on 30th September 1994.

A plaque recording two opening days, found abandoned in a skip at Chiswick, and believed to have been displayed at Bank. LT Museum 13605

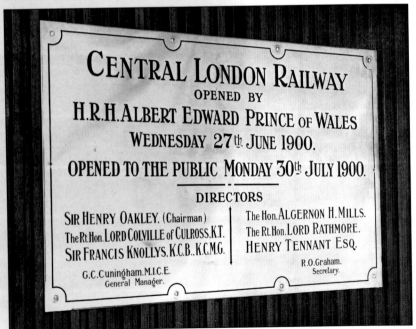